SASHIKO +
COLOR

stashBOOKS.

an imprint of C&T Publishing

SASHIKO + COLOR
First published in the United States in 2021 by Stash Books, an imprint of
C&T Publishing, Inc., P.O. Box 1456, Lafayette, CA 94549

IRO TO MOYO O TANOSHIMU SASHIKO NO KOMONO no. 4849
Copyright ©2019 Boutique-sha
Original Japanese edition published by Boutique-sha, Tokyo, Japan
English language rights, translation & production by World Book Media, LLC

Editing: Ayako Terashima and Kumiko Kosakai
Technical Editing: Tomomi Ahiko
Photography: Akane Kubota and Yoshihiko Koshizuka
Book Design: Kayo Koike and Yoko Maki
Tracing: Tamami Ozaki
Editor: Hitomi Takahashi
Publisher: Naito Akira

English Translation: Mayumi Anzai
English Language Editor: Lindsay Fair
English Edition Design: Stacy Wakefield Forte

ISBN: 978-1-64403-107-0

Manufactured in China

10 9 8 7 6 5 4 3 2 1

CONTENTS

✕ RIBBON HAND TOWEL

Brighten up your kitchen with this whimsical towel
stitched with a bold red design. The rhythmical pattern
was inspired by loops of curled ribbon.

INSTRUCTIONS ON PAGE 38 ⁄ DESIGN: SASHIKONAMI

✕ CROSS COASTERS

These minimalist coasters are inspired by classic Scandinavian design. Change the color of the fabric or sashiko thread to create an entirely different impression even when stitching the same pattern!

✷ DAISY CLOTH

This cheerful design features sunny yellow flowers on a crisp white background. Use this small stitchery as a pretty handkerchief, napkin, or table mat. Because it stitches up so quickly, this project makes for a great gift!

INSTRUCTIONS ON PAGE 44 ✎
DESIGN: SASHIKONAMI

For a fun twist, use bright yellow fabric for the backing.

PASSING STITCH POT HOLDER

This handy pot holder features an elegant color combination of dark brown and white thread on a rosy pink background. The unique passing stitch pattern may look intricate, but is actually suitable for beginners and works up quickly.

INSTRUCTIONS ON PAGE 47 DESIGN: SASHIKONAMI

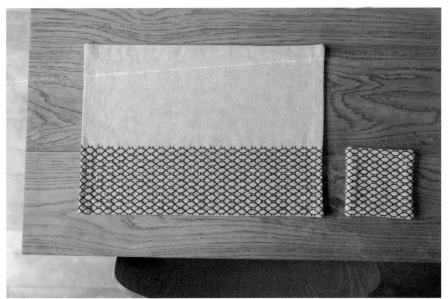

✂ PASSING STITCH PLACEMAT & COASTER SET

This coordinating table set features bold red waves created by weaving the thread through a framework of brown stitches. This modern combination will add a punch of color to any table setting.

INSTRUCTIONS ON PAGE 58 ✁ DESIGN: YUKO

✕ CIRCLE FUROSHIKI WRAP

This timeless circle motif showcases the beauty of simplicity and is perfectly suited for *furoshiki*, a traditional Japanese wrapping cloth.

· HOW TO WRAP WITH FUROSHIKI ·

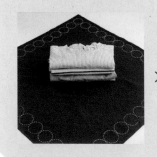  

⋇ CIRCLE TOTE BAG

Arrange oversize circles in a striking figure eight pattern to dress up a basic tote bag. This tote is the perfect size for carrying paperwork, grocery items, and everyday essentials.

INSTRUCTIONS ON PAGE 63 ⋰
DESIGN: YUKO

✕ COLORFUL CLASP PURSE

Embellish a simple clasp purse with an eyecatching zigzag design.
This petite purse is perfect for storing eyeglasses, pencils, or receipts.

INSTRUCTIONS ON PAGE 69 ⁄ DESIGN: SHOKO NISHIMURA

INSTRUCTIONS ON PAGE 93
DESIGN: SASHIKONAMI

✳ DRAWSTRING POUCH

This simple yet refreshing flower pattern is composed of stitches worked in four directions: vertical, horizontal, right diagonal, and left diagonal! Sew a few straight seams to transform the cloth into a beautiful drawstring pouch.

13

Stow the zip pouch inside the tote to help stay organized.

INSTRUCTIONS ON PAGES 73 & 75 ╱ DESIGN: SASHIKONAMI

✕ FLOWER CROSS TOTE & ZIP POUCH

This coordinating set features a beautiful flower cross pattern stitched in dark blue thread on a white background. Use the tote as a chic, modern everyday bag, while the zip pouch makes a great cosmetic case.

Use the cute little zip pouch to store lipstick and a compact.

✕ BOXY POUCH

Known as the persimmon flower, this striking geometric pattern replicates the appearance and texture of woven fabric when stitched across the entire surface of a project.

INSTRUCTIONS ON PAGE 78 ✧ DESIGN: ASAKO MORIOKA

✕ DOT PATTERN TOTE BAG

Combine simple running stitch and French knots to create a lyrical, dynamic pattern. This crowd-pleasing design will appeal to a variety of personal styles.

INSTRUCTIONS ON PAGE 82
DESIGN: ASAKO MORIOKA

For a special detail, extend the stitching onto the base of the bag. This will provide structure and add an unexpected design element.

17

✕ BISCORNU PIN CUSHIONS

These octagonal pin cushions may look complicated, but they are actually made from two squares of cloth. Have fun experimenting with color combinations to stitch up this eye-catching cross motif.

INSTRUCTIONS ON PAGE 88 ✕ DESIGN: AKIKO NISHIMURA

✂ BUTTON BROOCHES

These adorable brooches make great gifts. Personalize the pattern—try zigzags, crosses, or dashed lines—and the color scheme to suit the recipient's style.

B

A

C

INSTRUCTIONS ON PAGE 91 ✁
DESIGN: ASAKO MORIOKA

✕ STAR LUNCH BAG

Add a touch of sophistication to a
sack lunch with this handmade bag.
When stitched in a bright color, such
as the vibrant pink shown here, the
dazzling star motif bursts into life.

METAL CLASP COIN PURSE

This adorable miniature coin purse is a wonderful canvas for your favorite sashiko design. Try an arrangement of a few persimmon leaf motifs for sophisticated, understated style.

INSTRUCTIONS ON PAGE 102
DESIGN: ASAKO MORIOKA

⟨ RUNNING STITCH HAND TOWEL

Blue and yellow thread combine to create a summery hand towel that will be like a breath of fresh air in any kitchen. Composed entirely of running stitch, this design works up quickly and can even be added to a store-bought towel.

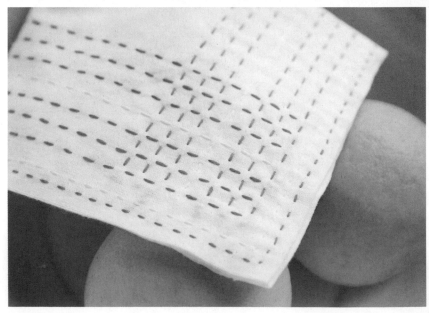

✕ LEAF HAND TOWEL

This refreshing blue and yellow leaf pattern
was inspired by cloisonné. This small towel
is ideal for covering a breadbasket or for use
as a handkerchief.

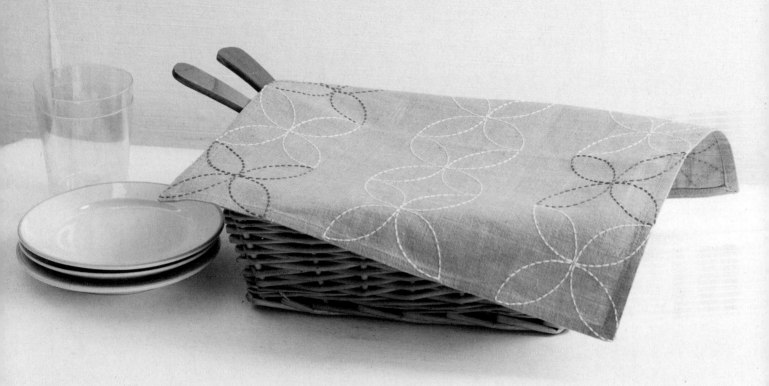

INSTRUCTIONS ON PAGE 107 ⁄ **DESIGN: HAKO YOSHIMURA**

✕ PICNIC BASKET CLOTH

This large, multipurpose cloth is the perfect picnic accessory—
use it to cover your basket during transport, then unfold it and
use it to serve the food when you're ready to eat. Use a checkered
fabric on one side and a solid fabric on the other to make the
cloth reversible and showcase the two-sided stitch pattern.

INSTRUCTIONS ON PAGE 109
DESIGN: YUKO

✂ TOOLS & MATERIALS ✂

Sashiko doesn't require fancy tools or equipment, but having the right supplies on hand will make the stitching process easier and more enjoyable. The following guide includes some basic information about sashiko and general embroidery supplies.

FABRIC

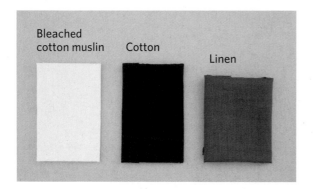

When stitching sashiko, opt for natural fibers, such as cotton and linen. Look for plain weave fabrics with a lower thread count. Ideal sashiko fabrics are slightly heavier than quilting weight fabrics—you don't want the fabric to be too thick or it will be difficult to stitch; nor do you want the fabric to be too thin as the threads on the back side may show through. You can also purchase bleached or unbleached cotton muslin, which works well for tea towels.

· PREPARING YOUR FABRIC ·

Fabric (ws)

Prewash your fabric before you start stitching in order to prevent shrinkage, wrinkles, and distortion. After washing and drying your fabric, make sure that the grain is straight and iron it from the wrong side.

THREAD

Sashiko thread is made from long staple cotton, which makes it strong and durable. Depending upon the manufacturer, it may be sold in skeins or on paper bobbins. It is available in several different weights, including fine, medium, and thick. The projects in this book use one or two strands, depending on the fabric weight and overall design.

NEEDLES

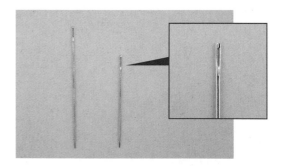

Sashiko needles are available in different lengths, but in general, they are long, rigid, and sharp. Long needles allow you to load multiple stitches onto the needle before pulling it through the fabric, allowing you to stitch straight lines very quickly. Shorter needles are easier for beginners to handle and are useful for stitching curves. Select your needle based on your thread, fabric weight, and personal preferences.

THIMBLE

Unlike traditional sewing thimbles, sashiko thimbles are worn at the base of your finger and feature a pad to help push the needle through the fabric. They are available in both leather and metal—both versions feature little dimples on the pad to help grip the needle.

PINS & PIN CUSHION

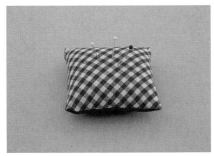

Use sewing pins to help hold a template in place when transferring a design onto fabric and to hold fabric pieces together during the construction of projects.

SCISSORS

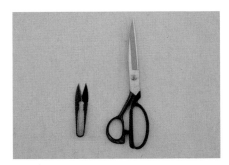

You'll need a pair of thread snips to clip threads and a pair of fabric scissors to cut cloth.

TRANSFER TOOLS

A **RULER:** Use a transparent ruler to draw guidelines and linear patterns, and to help cut fabric.

B **GRAPH PAPER:** Use to design your own sashiko patterns.

C **TRACING PAPER:** Use to copy designs from the book.

D **CELLOPHANE OR PLASTIC SHEET:** A sheet of thin plastic is useful when transferring designs onto fabric using the process shown on page 29. It isn't absolutely necessary, but it protects the tracing paper and makes the process smoother. You can even use a piece of thin plastic packaging as a substitute for cellophane.

E **CARD STOCK:** Use to make templates for curved designs (see page 28).

F **WATER SOLUBLE MARKING PEN:** Use this type of marking pen for drawing designs directly on fabric. Always test the pen on a scrap of fabric first to make sure the ink disappears as intended.

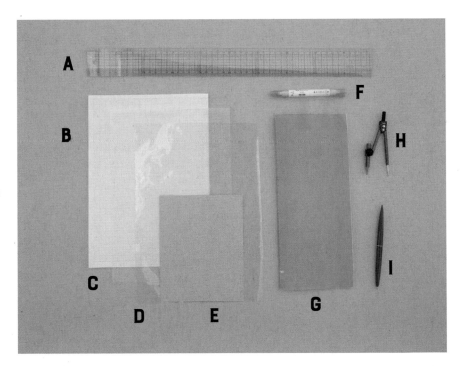

G **DRESSMAKERS CARBON PAPER:** Use this special paper to transfer designs onto fabric using the process shown on page 29. Use water to remove any stray marks.

H **COMPASS:** Use to draw curved patterns.

I **TRACER PEN:** Use to transfer designs onto fabric in conjunction with dressmakers carbon paper (see page 29). You can also use an empty ballpoint pen.

⚒ BASIC SASHIKO TECHNIQUES ⚒

The following guide explains the basic techniques for getting started stitching sashiko, including how to transfer designs onto fabric, how to prepare the thread, and how to stitch.

HOW TO TRANSFER DESIGNS ONTO FABRIC

As with any type of embroidery, there are many different methods that can be used to transfer designs onto fabric. Here, we'll illustrate three different options used for the projects in this book. Choose the option that best suits your individual project and personal preferences.

METHOD 1: DRAW DIRECTLY ON THE FABRIC

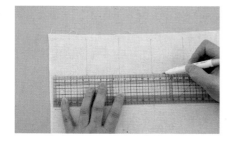
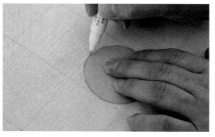
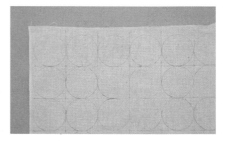

1   Use a transparent ruler and a water soluble marking pen to draw grid lines on the fabric.

2   Use the water soluble marking pen to draw the pattern, using the grid lines for reference. When drawing designs featuring curves, make a template out of card stock, then trace the template.

3   Completed view of the design once it has been transferred onto the fabric.

· TIP ·

If your design is complicated, it may help to erase the grid lines in order to make the stitching lines more visible. Once the entire design has been transferred, erase any unnecessary grid lines using a cotton swab dipped in water or an eraser pen.

METHOD 2: USE DRESSMAKERS CARBON PAPER

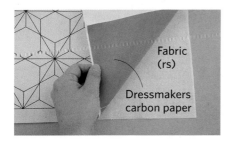

1 Photocopy the pattern from the book or copy it onto tracing paper. Next, align the dressmakers carbon paper with the right side of the fabric, making sure the chalk side is facing down. Position the copied pattern on top of the dressmakers carbon paper.

2 Layer the cellophane on top, then use a tracer pen to trace the pattern on top of the cellophane. For best results, use a ruler when tracing designs with straight lines.

3 Check to make sure all the lines transferred and correct any omissions if necessary.

· TIP ·

Even when using this method, it may be helpful to make a card stock template for curved design elements in order to achieve smooth lines.

METHOD 3: TRACE DIRECTLY ONTO THE FABRIC

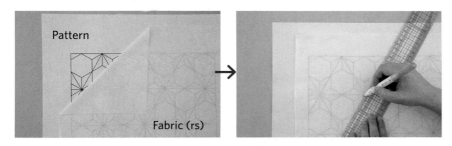

If you're using white or other light colored fabric, you can trace the design directly onto the fabric. Align the fabric on top of the pattern (you may want to photocopy it or trace it onto a sheet of paper so it lays flat). Use a water soluble marking pen to trace the design onto the fabric. As with the other transfer methods, use a ruler to trace the straight lines and make card stock templates for the curves.

HOW TO PREPARE THE THREAD

Before you can get started stitching, you'll need to prepare your thread. Taking a few minutes to get set up properly will make for a smoother stitching process.

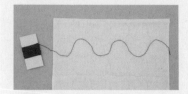

· A NOTE ON · THREAD LENGTH

As a general rule, your thread should be twice as long as the line you plan to stitch, plus 4 in (10 cm). Make sure that your thread isn't too long, as this may cause it to tangle while you stitch.

METHOD 1: WIND THREAD AROUND A BOBBIN

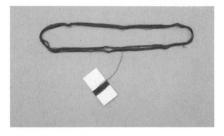

1 Unwind the skein so the thread is in a large loop. Wrap the thread around a small piece of card stock.

2 Cut a small slit at the edge of the card stock. Insert the thread end into the slit to keep the thread secure and tidy.

METHOD 2: CUT THREAD INTO CONVENIENT LENGTHS

1 Unwind the skein so the thread is in a large loop. Use scraps of thread to tie the bundle together in two different places.

2 Cut one end of the loop.

3 Remove individual lengths of thread from the bundle by pulling from the looped end.

HOW TO THREAD THE NEEDLE

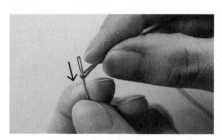

1 Fold the thread around the needle. Pull the needle against the thread to create a crease.

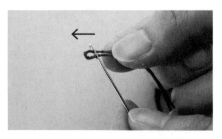

2 Insert the folded thread through the eye of the needle.

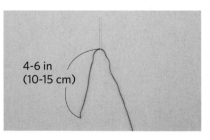

4-6 in (10-15 cm)

3 Pull the folded thread through the eye so the needle is 4-6 in (10-15 cm) from the end of the thread.

HOW TO STITCH SASHIKO

Sashiko designs are created using running stitch, a basic embroidery stitch composed of small, straight stitches positioned at a regular distance. In sashiko, the running stitch is worked by holding the needle still and making a pleating motion with the fabric to load several stitches onto the needle at once before pulling the thread through. Running stitch is very simple, but there are a few things to keep in mind when creating sashiko projects.

HOW TO WORK THE RUNNING STITCH

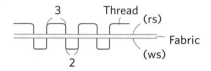

The stitches should be slightly longer on the right side of the work than on the wrong side—aim for a 3:2 stitch length ratio on right side vs. wrong side. The actual length of your stitches will depend on the motif you are stitching and the thickness of your fabric. For most of the projects in this book, you'll want to make your stitches ⅛–¼ in (3–5 mm) long. If your stitches are too small, they'll get lost in the fabric. If they're too long, it will be harder to see the overall design of the motif. The key is to make your stitches as uniform as possible.

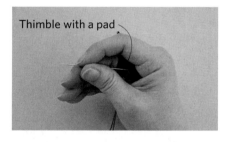

1 Use a thimble with a pad, especially when stitching thick fabric or using a long needle. Wear the thimble at the base of your middle finger on your dominant hand. Use your thumb and index finger to direct the needle and use the pad of the thimble to push the needle through the fabric.

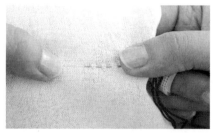

2 Insert the needle through to the right side of the fabric. Position the eye of the needle against the thimble pad and hold the needle and fabric between your thumb and index finger. Use your other hand to move the fabric up and down, placing it onto the needle using a pleating motion. This will load several stitches onto the needle at once and help ensure nice, straight stitching.

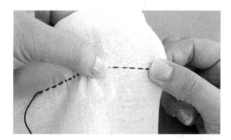

3 Once you have a few stitches loaded on the needle, use the thimble to push the needle through the fabric and pull the thread all the way through. The fabric will have scrunched up during the stitching process. Give the fabric a gentle tug to smooth it out and adjust the tension of the stitches. You can also use your fingertip to smooth out the stitches—just be careful not to snag the thread or fabric with your fingernail.

> ## · TIP ·
>
> The running stitch is really quite simple, but you may want to practice the motion of loading the stitches onto the needle to master the technique. This will help you get comfortable before you start a project and will make the stitching process quicker and more fluid.

HOW TO START & FINISH STITCHING

METHOD 1 MAKE A QUILTER'S KNOT

Use this method when stitching projects that will be finished with a backing fabric later.

TO START

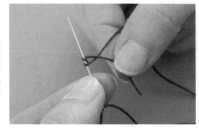

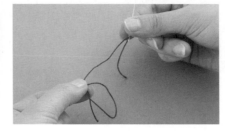

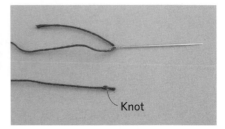

1 Hold a threaded needle between your thumb and index finger. Wrap the end of the thread around the needle twice.

2 Hold the wrapped thread in place with one hand. Use your other hand to pull the needle. The entire length of the thread should pass through your hands and the wraps should move to the end of the thread.

3 Pull the thread taut to form a knot at the end of the thread. Trim any excess thread beneath the knot.

TO FINISH

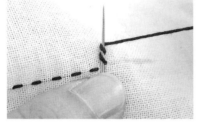

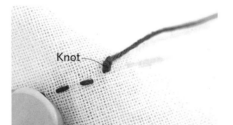

1 Align the needle against the fabric where the thread was last drawn out. Use your thumb to hold the needle in place and wrap the thread around it twice.

2 Hold the wrapped thread in place with one hand. Use your other hand to pull the needle. A knot should form close to the surface of the fabric. Trim the excess thread near the knot.

METHOD 2: HIDE THE KNOT

Use this method when stitching projects that have multiple layers of fabric, such as a hand towel.

TO START

1 Make a quilter's knot at the end of the thread as shown above. Insert the needle between the two layers of fabric and draw it out at the starting point.

2 Pull the thread to hide the knot between the two layers of fabric.

TO FINISH

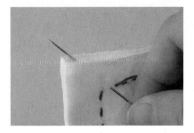

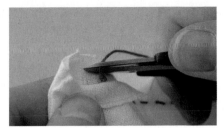

1 Insert the needle between the two layers of fabric when making your final stitch.

2 Pull the thread through to complete the final stitch. Align the needle against the fabric where the thread was last drawn out. Wrap the thread around the needle twice. Hold the wrapped thread in place with one hand and use your other hand to pull the needle.

3 A knot should form close to the surface of the fabric. Trim the excess thread near the knot.

METHOD 3: OVERLAP STITCHES

With this method, you'll overlap a few stitches at the beginning and end to secure the thread without a knot.

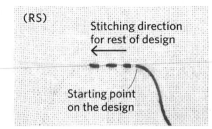

(RS) Stitching direction for rest of design

Starting point on the design

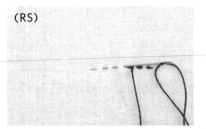

(RS)

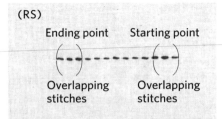

(RS) Ending point Starting point

Overlapping stitches   Overlapping stitches

1 Draw the needle out on the right side of the fabric about three stitches to the left of the starting point for the design. Working from left to right, make three stitches and draw the thread out at the starting point. For best results, make the third stitch slightly shorter than the others before drawing the needle out at the starting point.

2 Reverse direction and stitch on top of the three stitches made in step 1, working from right to left. Continue stitching the sashiko design.

3 When you reach the end of the stitching line, draw the needle out on the wrong side of the fabric. Working from the wrong side, overlap the final three stitches by scooping only the fabric so that these stitches are hidden underneath the main stitches. Note: It helps to make the first overlap stitch shorter.

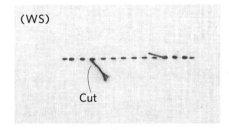

(WS)

Cut

4 Trim the excess thread, leaving about ⅛ in (3 mm). Be careful not to cut the thread too short or else the end may pop out on the right side of the work.

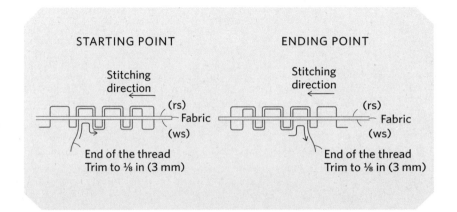

STARTING POINT

Stitching direction

(rs) Fabric
(ws)

End of the thread Trim to ⅛ in (3 mm)

ENDING POINT

Stitching direction

(rs) Fabric
(ws)

End of the thread Trim to ⅛ in (3 mm)

HOW TO ADD A NEW THREAD

If you run out of thread in the middle of stitching a sashiko design, you'll need to add a new thread. Select one of the methods illustrated below based on your individual project. Note: The photos below use two different colors of thread for visual clarity to help you see the old thread vs. the new thread.

METHOD 1: WHEN STITCHING A PROJECT WITHOUT A BACKING

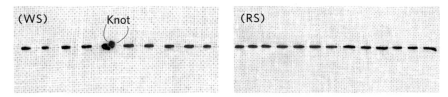

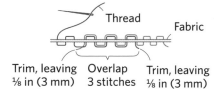

Rather than tying a knot, use the new thread to overlap the final three stitches made with the old thread. To overlap the stitches, work from the wrong side and scoop only the fabric so that the stitches made with the new thread are hidden underneath the final three stitches made with the old thread.

METHOD 2: WHEN STITCHING A PROJECT WITH A BACKING

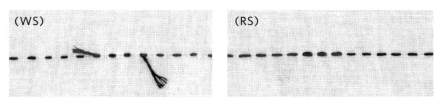

Make quilter's knots to finish the old thread and start the new thread (see page 32).

· HOW TO CARRY THE THREAD ·
ACROSS THE BACK OF THE WORK

For projects that will be finished with a backing fabric, you can carry the thread on the wrong side of the work to move to another area of the design rather than starting a new thread. Just make sure to leave a small loop rather than pulling the thread taut. Try to keep the loop smaller than 1 in (2.5 cm) otherwise, it may get caught or tangled.

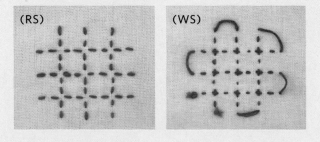

HOW TO STITCH CURVES

For gentle curves, try to keep your stitching line as straight as possible. For tight curves, draw the needle through the fabric after making 2–3 stitches and smooth out the thread. Continue with this process, making 2–3 stitches at a time and taking care not to stretch the fabric.

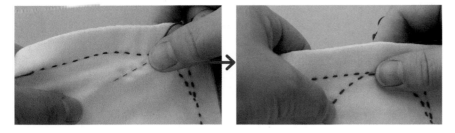

HOW TO STITCH CORNERS

Stitch the corner so that a stitch starts or ends right at the point, as shown in the photo below. Continue stitching along the next side. After you've worked several stitches, insert the needle under the corner stitch and pull the thread taut. This will adjust the tension at the corner without distorting the stitches. Remove the needle and continue stitching.

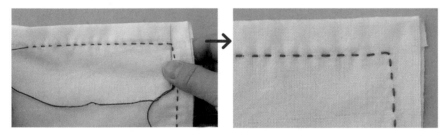

HOW TO STITCH NEATLY

The key to neat sashiko is to leave a small gap between stitches at the intersections of lines. Use the following tips to stitch different patterns you'll encounter in sashiko.

HOW TO STITCH A T

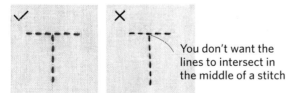

You don't want the lines to intersect in the middle of a stitch

The vertical line should intersect the horizontal line at a gap between stitches.

HOW TO STITCH A CORNER

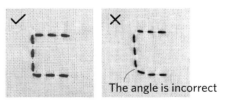

The angle is incorrect

Make sure stitches start or end right at the corner points in order to achieve right angles.

HOW TO STITCH A CROSS

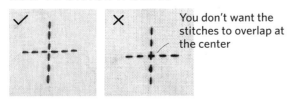

You don't want the stitches to overlap at the center

Make sure to leave a gap at the center where the horizontal and vertical lines intersect.

HOW TO STITCH A STAR

Leave a gap at the center where all the lines intersect.

HOW TO READ THE SASHIKO DIAGRAMS

Each project in the book includes a full-size diagram showing how to stitch the sashiko motif. The following guide explains the different symbols and notes you'll see on the sashiko diagrams used in this book.

NOTE: This book features authentic sashiko designs from Japan which are based on grids that use the metric system. For the most accurate results, it is recommended that you draw your grids following the metric measurements provided in the individual project diagrams. You'll will just need to use a standard ruler rather than a quilting ruler to draw your grids. If you prefer to work in inches, please note that you may have to adjust the pattern as the resulting motif will have fewer repeats than pictured here.

EXAMPLE SASHIKO DIAGRAM

1 When determining placement, align the center or corner of the diagram with the center or corner of the area for sashiko. Note that some diagrams only represent part of the sashiko motif. If necessary, move the diagram to complete the entire motif.

2 Mark grid lines on your fabric following the dimensions noted in the diagram. Depending on the motif, you may want to trace the sashiko design too in order to make the stitching process easier. Some diagrams feature the full motif, while others only contain part.

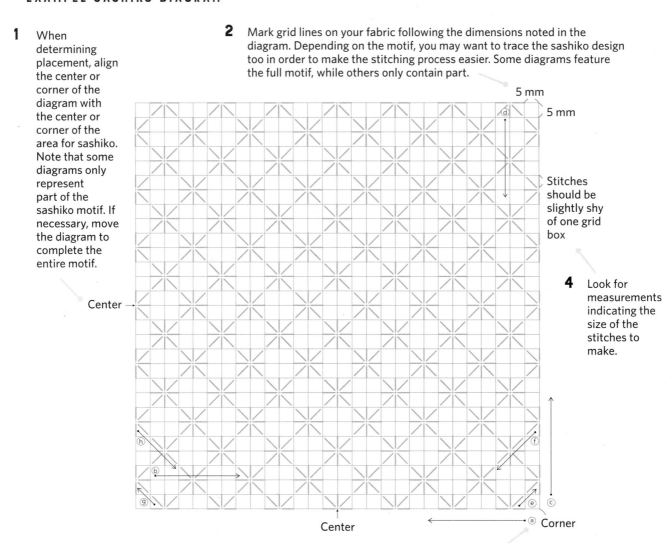

5 mm

5 mm

Stitches should be slightly shy of one grid box

Center →

4 Look for measurements indicating the size of the stitches to make.

Center

Corner

3 The circled letters and arrows indicate the stitching order and direction. Stitch each motif following the alphabetical order noted.

⟵•ⓐ = Stitch in the direction indicated by the arrow, following the order of the circled letters

⟵--•ⓐ = The dotted portion of the line indicates the thread will travel on the wrong side of the fabric

SASHIKO
PROJECTS

RIBBON HAND TOWEL

SHOWN ON PAGE 4

MATERIALS

+ FABRIC: 13½ × 28 in (34 × 71 cm) of unbleached cotton muslin
+ Thick sashiko thread in red

INSTRUCTIONS

1 Fold the fabric in half lengthwise with right sides together. Sew together along the top using ⅜ in (1 cm) seam allowance. Trim the seam allowance to ¼ in (7 mm).

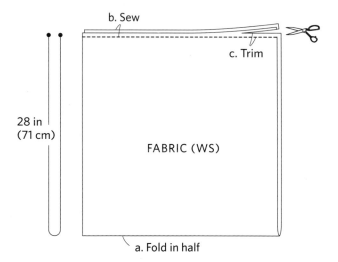

b. Sew

c. Trim

28 in (71 cm)

FABRIC (WS)

a. Fold in half

2 Turn right side out. Starting at the bottom right corner, work running stitch around the perimeter, stitching ⅜ in (1 cm) from the edge. Stitch through both layers of fabric and make the stitches about ⅛ in (2.5 mm) long.

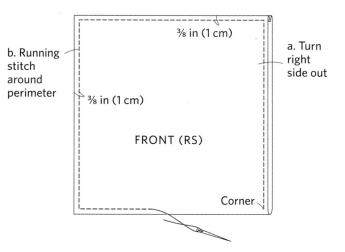

⅜ in (1 cm)

b. Running stitch around perimeter

a. Turn right side out

⅜ in (1 cm)

FRONT (RS)

Corner

3 Work passing stitch along the running stitch border from step 2.

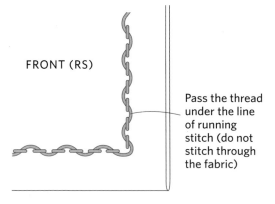

FRONT (RS)

Pass the thread under the line of running stitch (do not stitch through the fabric)

4 Mark 5 mm grid lines on the fabric. Stitch the motif as noted on page 39.

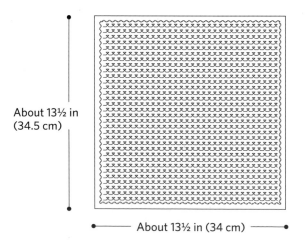

About 13½ in (34.5 cm)

About 13½ in (34 cm)

SASHIKO DIAGRAM

+ For best results, draw 5 mm grids. If you prefer to work in inches, draw ¼ in grids, but please note that you may have to adjust the pattern as the resulting motif will have fewer repeats than pictured here.

+ Stitch using a single strand of sashiko thread.

+ Follow the alphabetical order noted in the diagram.

5 mm

5 mm

Center →

Hide the thread between the two layers of fabric when moving from one row to the next.

Running stitches should be ⅛ in (2.5 mm) long

Stitch through both layers of fabric

Stitch through both layers of fabric

ⓓ

ⓕ

ⓔ

ⓒ

Center

ⓑ Pass the thread under the line of running stitch

Stitch through both layers of fabric

ⓐ

Corner

CROSS COASTERS

SHOWN ON PAGE 6

MATERIALS

FOR A

+ MAIN FABRIC: 5½ in (14 cm) square of beige linen
+ BACKING FABRIC: 6 in (15 cm) square of beige cotton/linen
+ FUSIBLE FLEECE: 5½ in (14 cm) square
+ 1½ in (4 cm) of 1 in (2.5 cm) wide linen tape
+ Fine sashiko thread in green

FOR B

+ MAIN FABRIC: 5½ in (14 cm) square of green linen
+ BACKING FABRIC: 6 in (15 cm) square of beige cotton/linen
+ FUSIBLE FLEECE: 5½ in (14 cm) square
+ 1½ in (4 cm) of 1 in (2.5 cm) wide linen tape
+ Fine sashiko thread in natural

INSTRUCTIONS

1 Mark 5 mm grid lines on the fabric. Stitch the motif as noted on page 42 (also refer to page 43). Once the stitching is complete, use the template to mark the finishing and cutting lines. Trim into a circle along the cutting line. This will be the front.

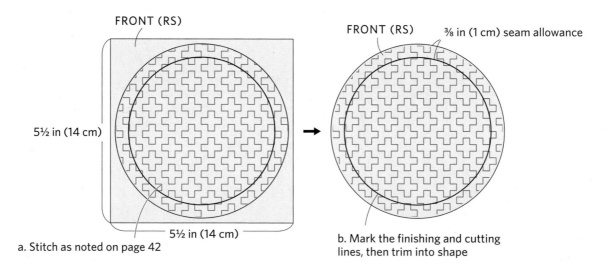

FRONT (RS)

5½ in (14 cm)

5½ in (14 cm)

a. Stitch as noted on page 42

FRONT (RS)

⅜ in (1 cm) seam allowance

b. Mark the finishing and cutting lines, then trim into shape

2 Adhere fusible fleece to the wrong side of the front. Fold the linen tape in half and baste to the right side of the front following the placement noted on the template.

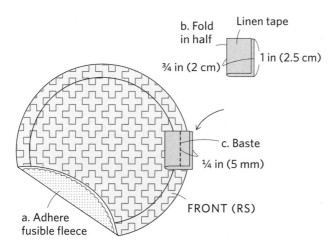

b. Fold in half

Linen tape

¾ in (2 cm)

1 in (2.5 cm)

c. Baste

¼ in (5 mm)

FRONT (RS)

a. Adhere fusible fleece

3 Cut two back pieces out of backing fabric. Sew the two back pieces with right sides together, leaving an opening as noted on the template. Press the seam allowance open.

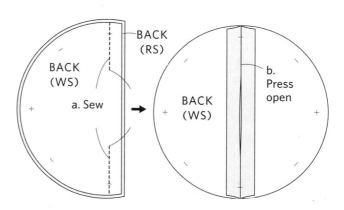

BACK (RS)

BACK (WS)

a. Sew

BACK (WS)

b. Press open

4 Sew the front and back with right sides together using ⅜ in (1 cm) seam allowance. Trim the excess fusible fleece, then make clips into the seam allowance around the entire circle.

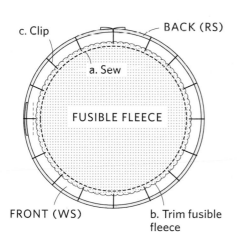

c. Clip

BACK (RS)

a. Sew

FUSIBLE FLEECE

FRONT (WS)

b. Trim fusible fleece

5 Turn the coaster right side out through the opening left in the back. Fold the seam allowances in and hand stitch the opening.

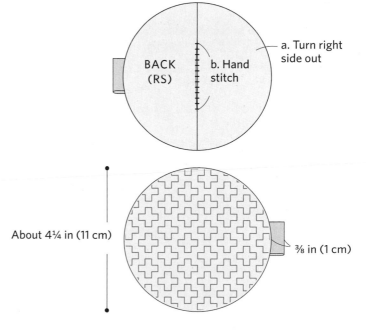

BACK (RS)

b. Hand stitch

a. Turn right side out

About 4¼ in (11 cm)

⅜ in (1 cm)

SASHIKO DIAGRAM & FULL-SIZE TEMPLATES

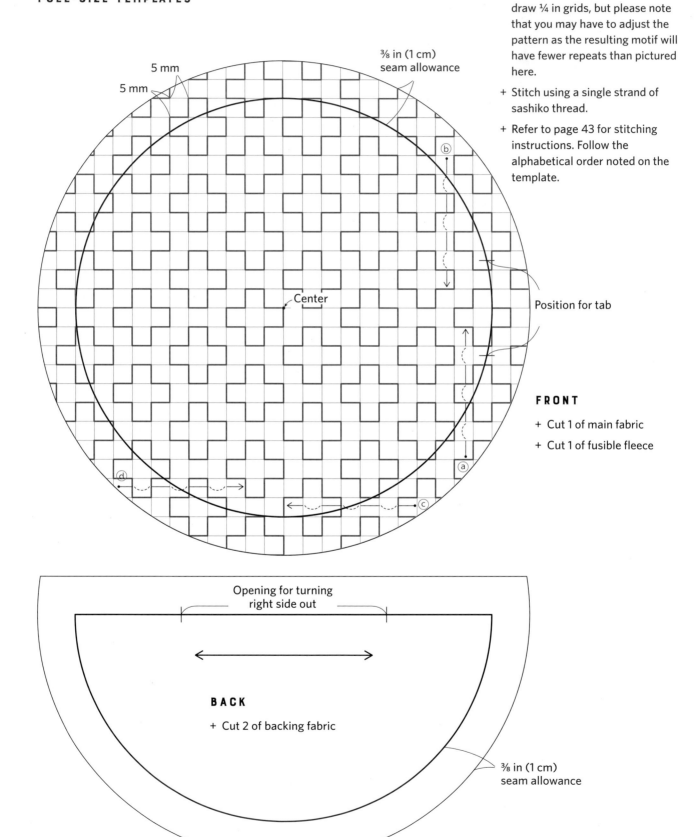

5 mm

5 mm

⅜ in (1 cm) seam allowance

+ For best results, draw 5 mm grids. If you prefer to work in inches, draw ¼ in grids, but please note that you may have to adjust the pattern as the resulting motif will have fewer repeats than pictured here.

+ Stitch using a single strand of sashiko thread.

+ Refer to page 43 for stitching instructions. Follow the alphabetical order noted on the template.

Center

ⓑ

Position for tab

ⓐ

ⓓ

ⓒ

FRONT

+ Cut 1 of main fabric

+ Cut 1 of fusible fleece

Opening for turning right side out

BACK

+ Cut 2 of backing fabric

⅜ in (1 cm) seam allowance

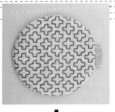
A

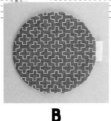
B

how to stitch the cross coasters

These coasters are made using single stitch, also known as running stitch. When working this stitch, use a longer needle.

1 Draw 5 mm square grid lines on the fabric using a water soluble marking pen. These grid lines will serve as a guide for stitching.

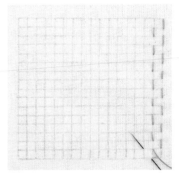

2 You'll use a single strand of sashiko thread to stitch this design. Start out by stitching the vertical rows (ⓐ and ⓑ). When the first row is complete, draw the needle out at the starting position of the next row and continue stitching.

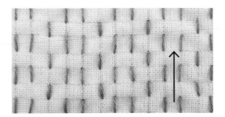

3 Continue stitching until all the vertical rows are complete.

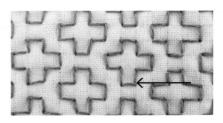

4 Next, stitch the horizontal rows (ⓒ and ⓓ), completing the individual cross motifs.

DAISY CLOTH

SHOWN ON PAGE 7

MATERIALS

+ FRONT FABRIC: 10 × 20 in (25 × 50 cm) of unbleached cotton muslin
+ BACKING FABRIC: 10 in (25 cm) square of yellow cotton double gauze
+ Sashiko thread in yellow

INSTRUCTIONS

1 Cut two 9½ in (24 cm) squares of unbleached cotton muslin. Mark 5 mm grid lines on one of the pieces of fabric in the area noted below.

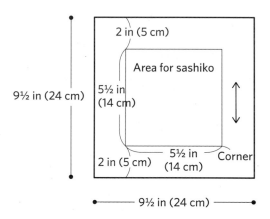

2 Layer the two squares on top of each other. Stitch the motif as noted on page 46 (also refer to page 45), stitching through both layers of fabric.

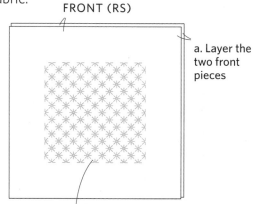

3 Trim into an 8¾ in (22 cm) square, keeping the sashiko design centered. This will be the front.

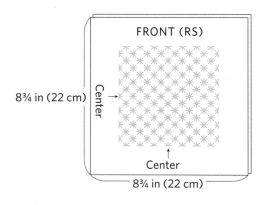

4 Cut an 8¾ in (22 cm) square of yellow cotton double gauze for the back. Sew the front and back with right sides together, using ⅜ in (1 cm) seam allowance. Leave a 2½ in (6 cm) opening along one side. Trim the corner seam allowances at an angle.

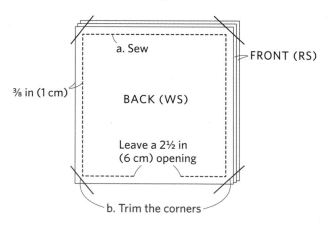

5 Turn right side out. Running stitch around the perimeter, stitching ¼ in (7 mm) from the edge. Stitch through all three layers of fabric and make the stitches about ¼ in (6 mm) long. See the diagram below for tips on hiding the knots.

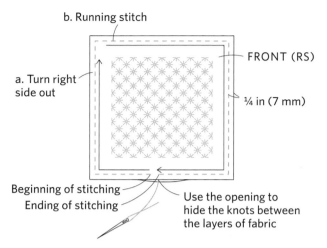

b. Running stitch

FRONT (RS)

a. Turn right side out

¼ in (7 mm)

Beginning of stitching
Ending of stitching

Use the opening to hide the knots between the layers of fabric

6 Hand stitch the opening closed.

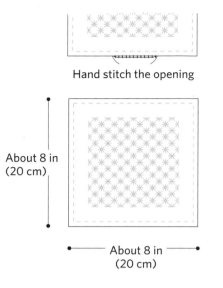

Hand stitch the opening

About 8 in (20 cm)

About 8 in (20 cm)

how to stitch the daisy cloth

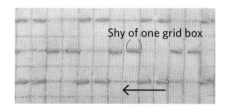

Shy of one grid box

1 Stitch the horizontal rows (ⓐ and ⓑ) first. Each stitch should be slightly shy of one grid box. Use a single strand of sashiko thread.

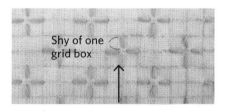

Shy of one grid box

2 Stitch the vertical rows (ⓒ and ⓓ) next. Make sure to leave a gap at the center where the vertical rows intersect the horizontal rows.

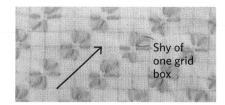

Shy of one grid box

3 Stitch the right diagonal rows (ⓔ and ⓕ) next.

Shy of one grid box

4 Finish by stitching the left diagonal rows (ⓖ and ⓗ). Again, make sure there is a gap where all the lines intersect.

SASHIKO DIAGRAM

+ For best results, draw 5 mm grids. If you prefer to work in inches, draw ¼ in grids, but please note that you may have to adjust the pattern as the resulting motif will have fewer repeats than pictured here.

+ Stitch using a single strand of sashiko thread.

+ Refer to page 45 for stitching instructions. Follow the alphabetical order noted in the diagram.

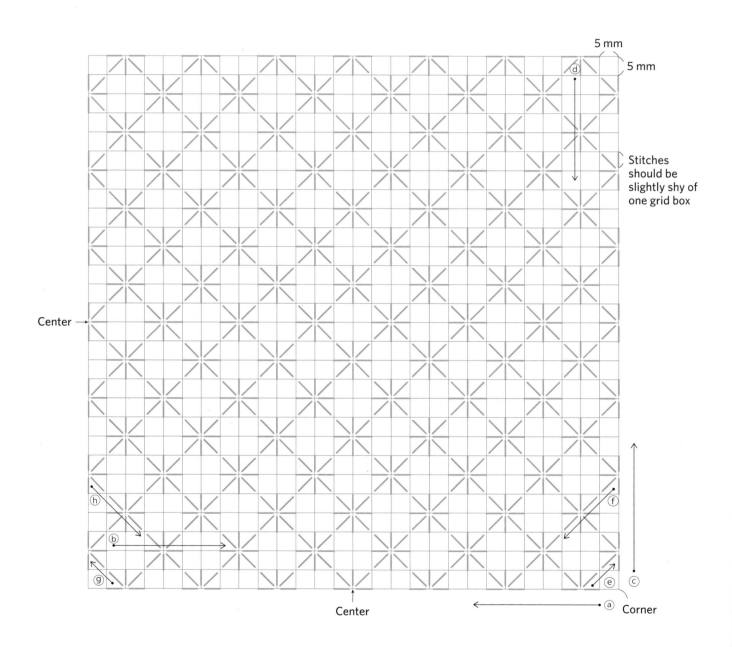

PASSING STITCH POT HOLDER

SHOWN ON PAGE 8

MATERIALS

+ LOWER FRONT FABRIC: 8 in (20 cm) square of pink linen
+ UPPER FRONT AND BACKING FABRIC: 8 × 10 in (20 × 25 cm) of beige linen
+ FUSIBLE FLEECE: 16 × 8 in (40 × 20 cm)
+ CORD: 2½ in (6 cm) of ⅛ in (3 mm) diameter round rope
+ Sashiko thread in dark brown
+ Fine sashiko thread in natural

INSTRUCTIONS

1 Cut a 7½ × 6 in (19 × 15.5 cm) rectangle of pink linen. Mark 5 mm grid lines on the fabric in the area noted below.

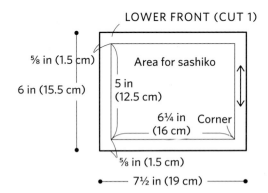

LOWER FRONT (CUT 1)

⅝ in (1.5 cm)

6 in (15.5 cm)

Area for sashiko

5 in (12.5 cm)

6¼ in (16 cm) Corner

⅝ in (1.5 cm)

7½ in (19 cm)

2 Stitch the motif as noted on page 49 (also refer to page 50). This will be the lower front.

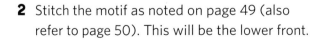

LOWER FRONT (RS)

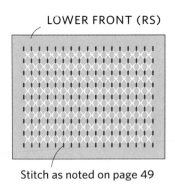

Stitch as noted on page 49

3 Mark the finishing lines following the dimensions noted below. Trim into a 6¾ × 5½ in (17 × 14 cm) rectangle, keeping the sashiko design centered.

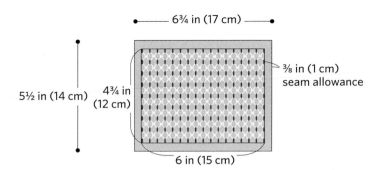

6¾ in (17 cm)

5½ in (14 cm)

4¾ in (12 cm)

⅜ in (1 cm) seam allowance

6 in (15 cm)

4 Cut a 6¾ × 2 in (17 × 5 cm) rectangle of beige linen for the upper front. Sew the upper and lower fronts with right sides together using ⅜ in (1 cm) seam allowance. Press the seam allowance open.

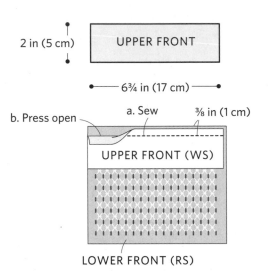

2 in (5 cm)

UPPER FRONT

6¾ in (17 cm)

b. Press open — a. Sew — ⅜ in (1 cm)

UPPER FRONT (WS)

LOWER FRONT (RS)

5 Form the 2½ in (6 cm) cord into a loop and baste to the front following the placement noted below.

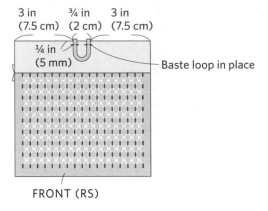

3 in (7.5 cm) ¾ in (2 cm) 3 in (7.5 cm)

¼ in (5 mm)

Baste loop in place

FRONT (RS)

6 Cut two 6¾ in (17 cm) squares of fusible fleece and one 6¾ in (17 cm) square of beige linen for the back. Align the front and back with right sides together, then position one square of fusible fleece on top and the other on the bottom. Sew together using ⅜ in (1 cm) seam allowance. Leave a 3 in (8 cm) opening along one side.

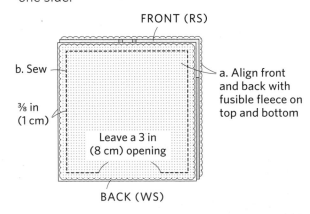

FRONT (RS)

b. Sew

⅜ in (1 cm)

a. Align front and back with fusible fleece on top and bottom

Leave a 3 in (8 cm) opening

BACK (WS)

7 Trim any excess fusible fleece from the seam allowance. Next, trim the corner seam allowances at an angle.

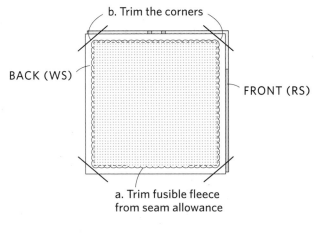

b. Trim the corners

BACK (WS)

FRONT (RS)

a. Trim fusible fleece from seam allowance

8 Turn right side out.
Hand stitch the
opening closed.

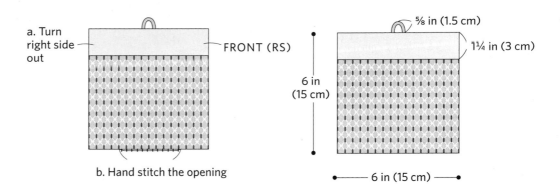

a. Turn right side out

FRONT (RS)

b. Hand stitch the opening

⅝ in (1.5 cm)

1¼ in (3 cm)

6 in (15 cm)

6 in (15 cm)

SASHIKO DIAGRAM

+ For best results, draw 5 mm grids. If you prefer to work in inches, draw ¼ in grids, but please note that you may have to adjust the pattern as the resulting motif will have fewer repeats than pictured here.

+ Stitch using a single strand of sashiko thread.

+ Refer to page 50 for stitching instructions. Follow the alphabetical order noted in the diagram.

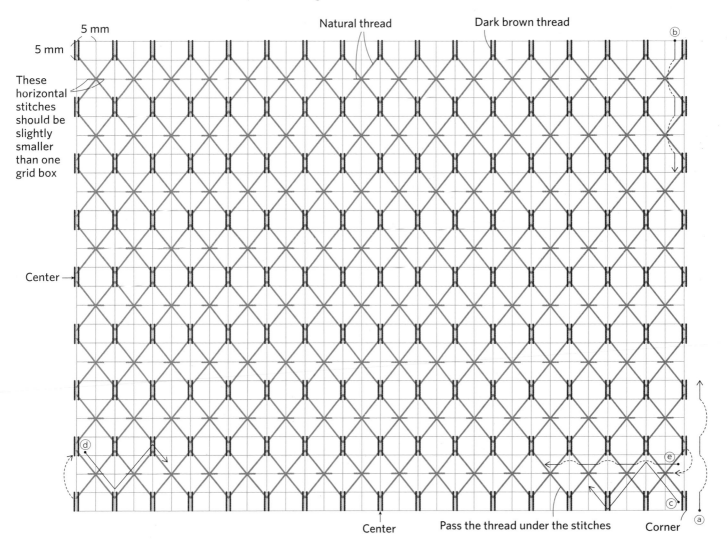

5 mm

5 mm

These horizontal stitches should be slightly smaller than one grid box

Natural thread

Dark brown thread

Center →

Center

Pass the thread under the stitches

Corner

how to stitch the passing stitch pot holder

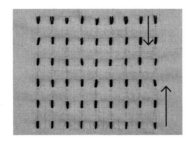

1 Start by stitching the vertical rows (ⓐ and ⓑ) using a single strand of dark brown sashiko thread. Make two separate stitches right next to each other as shown in the photo above.

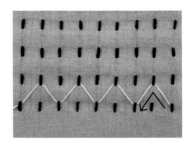

2 Next, you'll pass the a single strand of natural thread underneath the stitches from step 1 to create a zigzag pattern working from right to left (ⓒ).

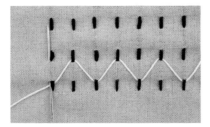

3 When you reach the left edge, insert the needle through to the wrong side of the fabric and draw it out one row above, right at the base of the first stitch of the second row.

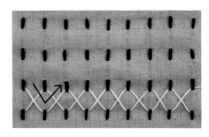

4 Pass the thread underneath the remaining stitches to create a zigzag pattern working from left to right (ⓓ). You'll be creating an X pattern.

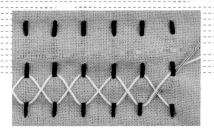

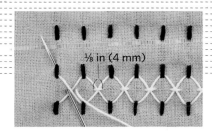

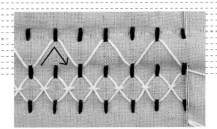

5 When you reach the right edge, insert the needle through to the wrong side of the fabric and draw it out in the middle of the first two rows of vertical stitches, just to the right of the first X.

6 Make short horizontal stitches to secure each X in place (ⓒ)—the stitches should be about ⅛ in (4 mm). When you reach the left edge, insert the needle through to the wrong side of the fabric and draw it out at the top of the first stitch of the second row.

7 Pass the thread under the stitches to create a zigzag pattern working from left to right. When you reach the right edge, insert the needle through to the wrong side of the fabric and draw it out one row above, right at the base of the first stitch of the third row.

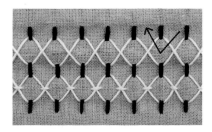

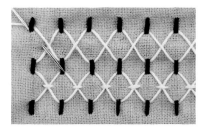

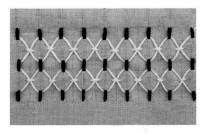

8 Pass the thread under the stitches to create a zigzag pattern working from right to left. You'll be completing the X pattern for this second row of passing stitch.

9 When you reach the left edge, insert the needle through to the wrong side of the fabric and draw it out in the middle of the second and third rows of vertical stitches, just to the left of the first cross.

10 Make short horizontal stitches to secure each X in place—the stitches should be about ⅛ in (4 mm). When you reach the right edge, insert the needle through to the wrong side of the fabric and draw it out at the top of the first stitch of the third row.

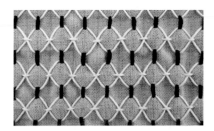

11 Repeat steps 2–10 to finish passing the thread under the remaining vertical stitches.

PASSING STITCH PLACEMAT & COASTER SET

SHOWN ON PAGE 9

MATERIALS

FOR THE PLACEMAT

+ FRONT FABRIC: 15¾ × 11¾ in (40 × 30 cm) of beige linen

+ BACK FABRIC: 15¾ × 11¾ in (40 × 30 cm) of beige cotton/linen

+ Sashiko thread in dark brown and red

FOR THE COASTER

+ FRONT FABRIC: 6 in (15 cm) square of beige linen

+ BACK FABRIC: 6 in (15 cm) square of beige cotton/linen

+ Sashiko thread in dark brown and red

INSTRUCTIONS

FOR THE PLACEMAT

1 Cut a 15½ × 11¼ in (39 × 28.5 cm) rectangle of beige linen. Mark 5 mm grid lines on the fabric in the area noted below.

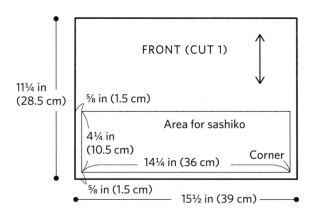

FRONT (CUT 1)

11¼ in (28.5 cm)

⅝ in (1.5 cm)

Area for sashiko

4¼ in (10.5 cm)

14¼ in (36 cm)

Corner

⅝ in (1.5 cm)

15½ in (39 cm)

2 Stitch the motif as noted on page 55 (also refer to page 56). Mark the finishing lines following the dimensions noted below. Trim into a 15 × 10¾ in (38 × 27 cm) rectangle, keeping the sashiko design centered. This will be the front.

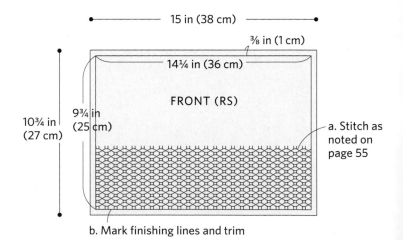

15 in (38 cm)

⅜ in (1 cm)

14¼ in (36 cm)

FRONT (RS)

9¾ in (25 cm)

10¾ in (27 cm)

a. Stitch as noted on page 55

b. Mark finishing lines and trim

3 Cut a 15 × 10¾ in (38 × 27 cm) rectangle of beige cotton/linen for the back. Sew the front and back with right sides together, using ⅜ in (1 cm) seam allowance. Leave a 4 in (10 cm) opening along one side. Trim the corner seam allowances at an angle.

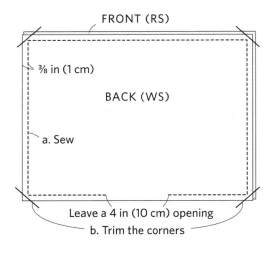

FRONT (RS)

⅜ in (1 cm)

BACK (WS)

a. Sew

Leave a 4 in (10 cm) opening

b. Trim the corners

4 Turn right side out and hand stitch the opening closed.

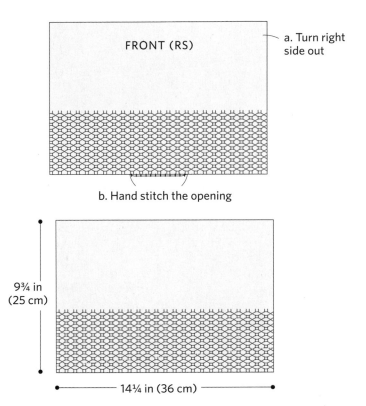

FRONT (RS)

a. Turn right side out

b. Hand stitch the opening

9¾ in (25 cm)

14¼ in (36 cm)

INSTRUCTIONS
FOR THE COASTER

1 Cut a 5¼ in (13.5 cm) square of beige linen. Mark 5 mm grid lines on the fabric in the area noted below.

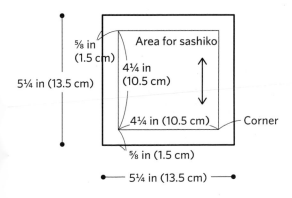

⅝ in (1.5 cm)

5¼ in (13.5 cm)

Area for sashiko

4¼ in (10.5 cm)

4¼ in (10.5 cm)

Corner

⅝ in (1.5 cm)

5¼ in (13.5 cm)

2 Stitch the motif as noted on page 55 (also refer to page 56). Mark the finishing lines following the dimensions noted below. Trim into a 4¾ in (12 cm) square, keeping the sashiko design centered. This will be the front.

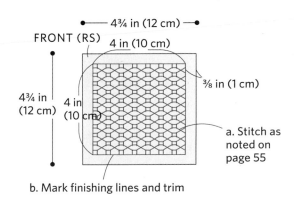

4¾ in (12 cm)

FRONT (RS)

4 in (10 cm)

⅜ in (1 cm)

4¾ in (12 cm)

4 in (10 cm)

a. Stitch as noted on page 55

b. Mark finishing lines and trim

3 Cut a 14½ × 10¾ in (37 × 27 cm) rectangle of beige cotton/linen for the back. Sew the front and back with right sides together, using ⅜ in (1 cm) seam allowance. Leave a 1½ in (4 cm) opening along one side. Trim the corner seam allowances at an angle.

4 Turn right side out and hand stitch the opening closed.

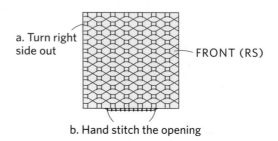

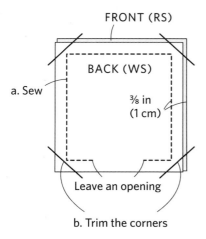

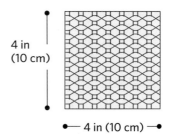

SASHIKO DIAGRAM

(for both placemat and coaster)

+ For best results, draw 5 mm grids. If you prefer to work in inches, draw ¼ in grids, but please note that you may have to adjust the pattern as the resulting motif will have fewer repeats than pictured here.

+ Stitch using a single strand of sashiko thread.

+ Refer to page 56 for stitching instructions. Follow the alphabetical order noted in the diagram.

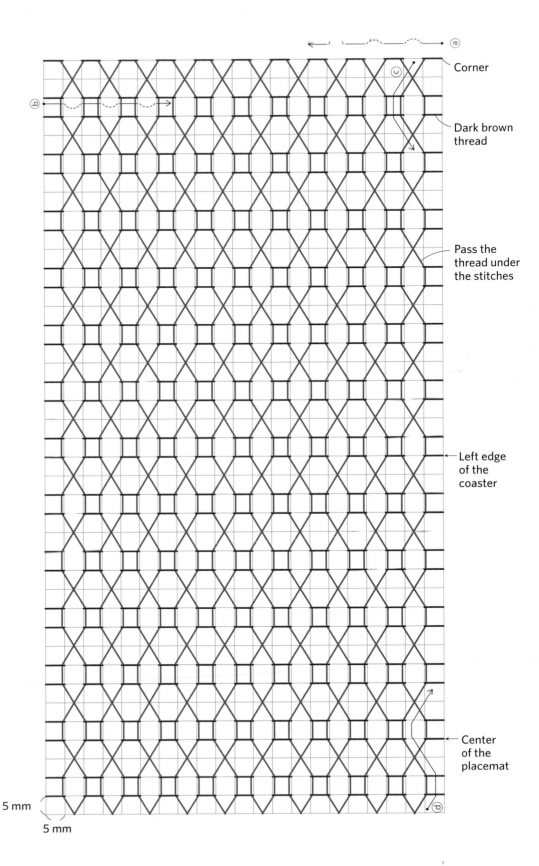

Corner

Dark brown thread

Pass the thread under the stitches

Left edge of the coaster

Center of the placemat

5 mm

5 mm

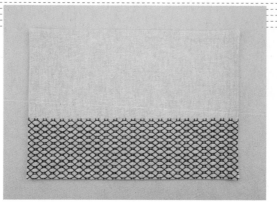
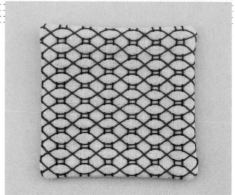

how to stitch the passing stitch placemat & coaster set

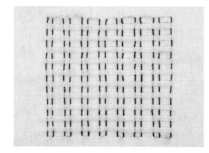

1 Stitch the vertical rows (ⓐ and ⓑ) using a single strand dark brown sashiko thread.

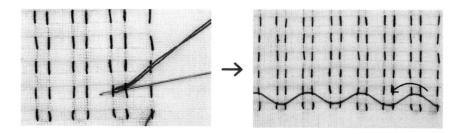

2 Pass a single strand of red sashiko thread underneath the vertical stitches from step 1 to create a wavy zigzag pattern working from right to left (ⓒ).

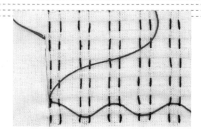 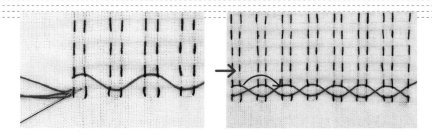 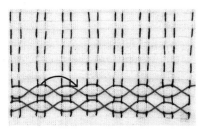

3 When you reach the left edge, insert the needle through to the wrong side of the fabric and draw it out one row below, right at the top of the first stitch of the first row.

4 Pass the thread underneath the remaining stitches to create a wavy zigzag pattern working from left to right (ⓓ). You'll be creating a cross pattern.

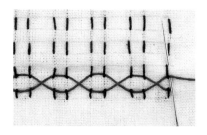 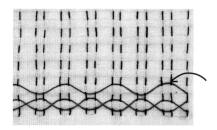

5 When you reach the right edge, insert the needle through to the wrong side of the fabric and draw it out one row above, right at the top of the first stitch of the second row.

6 Pass the thread underneath the stitches to create a wavy zigzag pattern working from right to left, just like in step 2.

7 When you reach the left edge, insert the needle through to the wrong side of the fabric and draw it out one row below, right at the top of the first stitch of the second row. Pass the thread underneath the remaining stitches to create a wavy zigzag pattern working from left to right, just like in step 4.

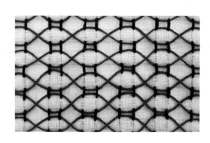

8 Repeat this process to finish passing the thread under the remaining vertical stitches.

CIRCLE FUROSHIKI WRAP

SHOWN ON PAGE 10

MATERIALS

+ FABRIC: 30 in (76 cm) square of red linen
+ Fine sashiko thread in tan

INSTRUCTIONS

1 Use the technique shown on page 59 to miter the corners and hem the edges of the fabric.

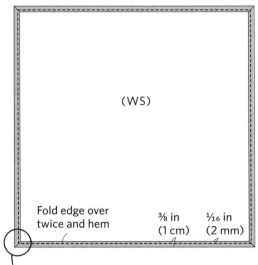

(WS)

Fold edge over twice and hem

⅜ in (1 cm)   ¹⁄₁₆ in (2 mm)

See page 59 for instructions on mitering corners

2 Transfer the sashiko template on page 62 onto the fabric in the area noted below.

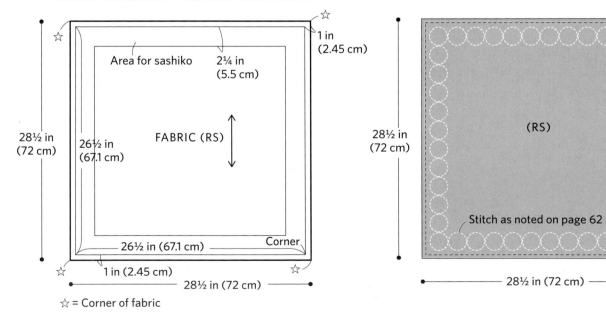

Area for sashiko   2¼ in (5.5 cm)

1 in (2.45 cm)

28½ in (72 cm)

26½ in (67.1 cm)

FABRIC (RS)

26½ in (67.1 cm)   Corner

1 in (2.45 cm)   28½ in (72 cm)

☆ = Corner of fabric

3 Stitch the motif as noted on page 60.

(RS)

28½ in (72 cm)

Stitch as noted on page 62

28½ in (72 cm)

how to miter the corners

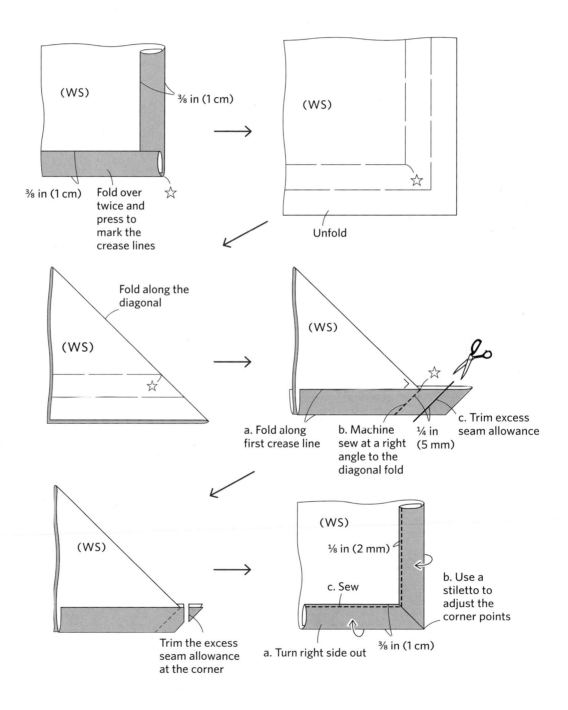

(WS)

⅜ in (1 cm)

⅜ in (1 cm)   Fold over twice and press to mark the crease lines

(WS)

Unfold

Fold along the diagonal

(WS)

(WS)

a. Fold along first crease line

b. Machine sew at a right angle to the diagonal fold

¼ in (5 mm)

c. Trim excess seam allowance

(WS)

Trim the excess seam allowance at the corner

(WS)

⅛ in (2 mm)

b. Use a stiletto to adjust the corner points

c. Sew

a. Turn right side out   ⅜ in (1 cm)

how to stitch the circle furoshiki wrap

The following guide shows how to stitch a circle motif. You'll stitch half of each circle, working from right to left, then reverse directions and complete each circle. You can use this technique for both projects that have a backing and those that don't.

1   Draw the needle out near the center top of the first circle (☆) without tying a knot. Leave a 4 in (10 cm) thread tail on the wrong side. Stitch ¾ of the circle, stopping at the 9 o'clock position.

2   Draw the needle out at the 3 o'clock position on the next circle. Stitch the upper half of the circle, stopping at the 9 o'clock position.

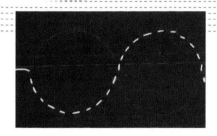 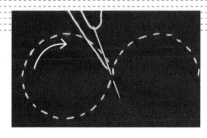 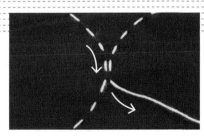

3 Follow this process to stitch half of each circle, alternating upper half and lower half each time.

4 Stitch the entire last circle. Next, you'll complete the remaining half of each circle, working from left to right. Draw the needle out on the right side to continue stitching the next circle.

5 Make sure the stitches are aligned where the two circles meet.

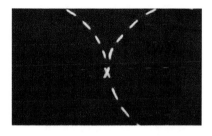 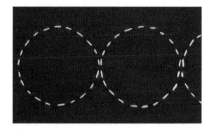 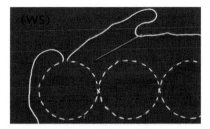

6 You'll see a cross on the wrong side of fabric where you move from one circle to the next.

7 Finish stitching the row of circles.

8 When you complete the final circle of the row, draw the thread out on the wrong side of the fabric.

 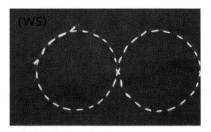

9 Secure the thread end by overlapping stitches so they aren't visible on the right side of the fabric (refer to page 33). Work back toward the starting point for 3-4 stitches.

> **· NOTE ·**
>
> The thread should not be visible on the right side of the fabric when you use the overlap method. It will be hidden underneath the existing stitches.

10 Trim the excess thread, leaving about $\frac{1}{16}$ in (2 mm). Make sure not to cut the thread too short otherwise it may pop out on the right side of the fabric.

+ For best results, draw 2.75 cm grids. If you prefer to work in inches, draw 1 in grids, but please note that you may have to adjust the pattern as the resulting motif will have fewer repeats than pictured here.

+ Stitch using a single strand of sashiko thread.

+ Refer to page 60 for stitching instructions. Follow the alphabetical order noted in the diagram.

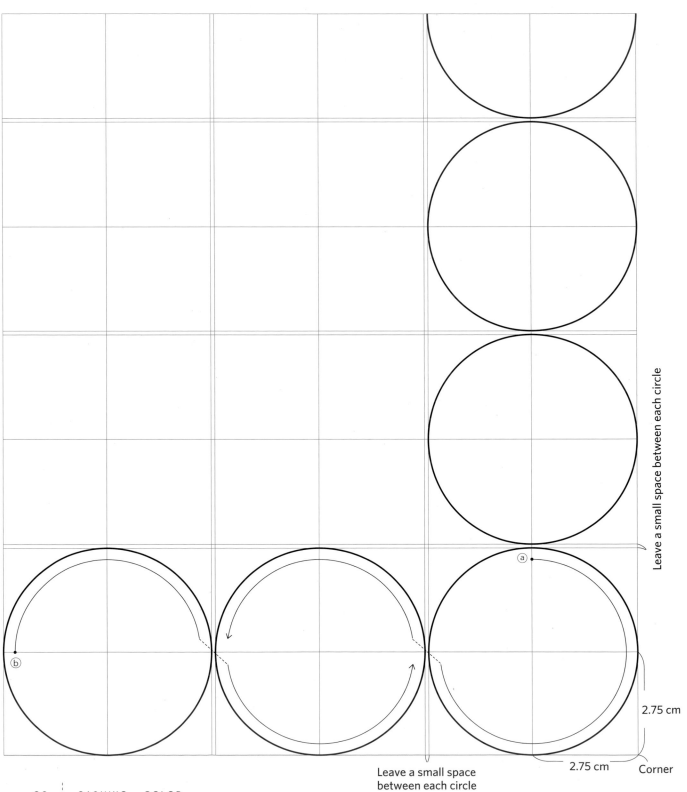

Leave a small space between each circle

2.75 cm

2.75 cm

Corner

Leave a small space between each circle

CIRCLE TOTE BAG

SHOWN ON PAGE 11

MATERIALS

+ OUTSIDE FABRIC: 19¾ × 23¾ in (50 × 60 cm) of navy blue linen
+ LINING FABRIC: 9¾ × 23¾ in (35 × 60 cm) of beige cotton/linen
+ Sashiko thread in off-white

INSTRUCTIONS

1 Cut a 9¾ × 23¾ in (25 × 60 cm) rectangle of navy blue linen for the bag outside. Transfer the sashiko template on page 68 onto the fabric in the area noted below. Note: The sashiko design will be stitched on both the front and back of the bag.

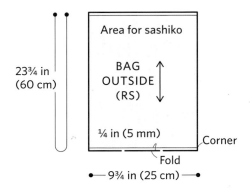

Area for sashiko

BAG OUTSIDE (RS)

23¾ in (60 cm)

¼ in (5 mm)

Corner

Fold

9¾ in (25 cm)

2 Stitch the motif as noted on page 66.

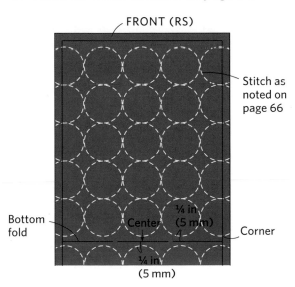

FRONT (RS)

Stitch as noted on page 66

Bottom fold

Center

¼ in (5 mm)

Corner

¼ in (5 mm)

3 Cut a 4¾ × 10¼ in (12 × 26 cm) rectangle of navy blue linen for the pocket. Transfer the sashiko template on page 68 onto the fabric in the area noted below. Note: Align the center bottom of the template with the center bottom of the pocket and copy two rows of the sashiko design as shown in the step 4 diagram.

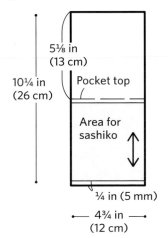

5⅛ in (13 cm)

Pocket top

10¼ in (26 cm)

Area for sashiko

¼ in (5 mm)

4¾ in (12 cm)

4 Stitch the motif on the pocket.

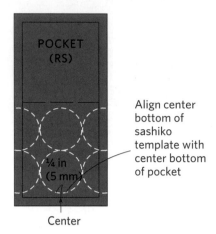

Align center bottom of sashiko template with center bottom of pocket

POCKET (RS)

¼ in (5 mm)

Center

5 Fold the bag outside in half with right sides together. Sew together along the left and right edges using ⅜ in (1 cm) seam allowance. Press the seams open.

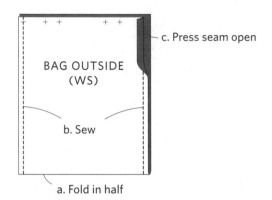

c. Press seam open

BAG OUTSIDE (WS)

b. Sew

a. Fold in half

6 Fold the pocket in half with right sides together. Sew around three sides, leaving a 2 in (5 cm) opening in one side. Trim the corner seam allowances at an angle. Turn right side out and hand stitch the opening closed.

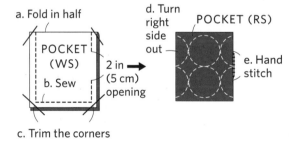

a. Fold in half

POCKET (WS)

b. Sew

2 in (5 cm) opening

d. Turn right side out

POCKET (RS)

e. Hand stitch

c. Trim the corners

7 Cut a 9¾ × 23¾ in (25 × 60 cm) rectangle of beige cotton/linen for the lining. Mark the pocket placement as noted below.

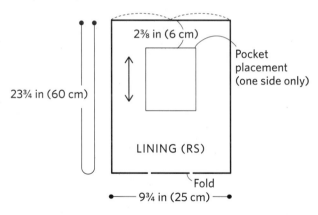

2⅜ in (6 cm)

Pocket placement (one side only)

23¾ in (60 cm)

LINING (RS)

Fold

9¾ in (25 cm)

8 Topstitch the pocket to the right side of the lining.

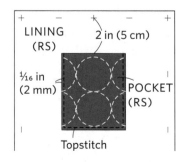

LINING (RS)

2 in (5 cm)

1/16 in (2 mm)

POCKET (RS)

Topstitch

9 Fold the lining in half with right sides together. Sew together along the left and right edges using ⅜ in (1 cm) seam allowance. Leave a 4 in (10 cm) opening in one side. Press the seams open.

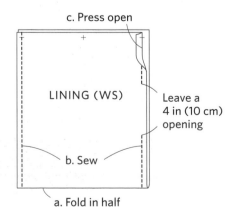

c. Press open

LINING (WS)

Leave a 4 in (10 cm) opening

b. Sew

a. Fold in half

10 Cut two 2½ × 17¼ in (6 × 44 cm) rectangles of navy blue linen for the handles. Fold and press the top and bottom edges over ¼ in (5 mm).

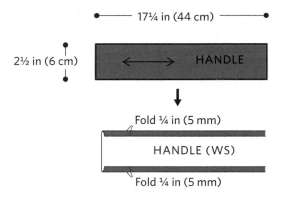

17¼ in (44 cm)

2½ in (6 cm)

HANDLE

Fold ¼ in (5 mm)

HANDLE (WS)

Fold ¼ in (5 mm)

11 Fold each handle in half. Topstitch along the top and bottom, stitching close to the edges.

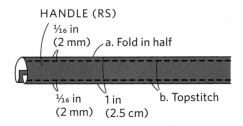

HANDLE (RS)

¹⁄₁₆ in (2 mm)

a. Fold in half

¹⁄₁₆ in (2 mm)

1 in (2.5 cm)

b. Topstitch

* Make 2 handles

12 Turn the bag outside right side out. Baste the handles to the bag outside following the placement noted below.

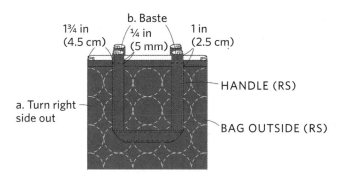

1¾ in (4.5 cm)

b. Baste ¼ in (5 mm)

1 in (2.5 cm)

a. Turn right side out

HANDLE (RS)

BAG OUTSIDE (RS)

13 Insert the bag outside into the lining with right sides together. Sew together around the bag opening.

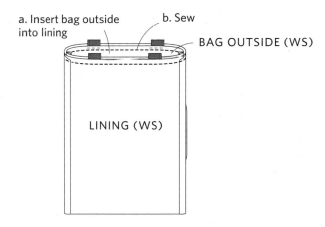

a. Insert bag outside into lining

b. Sew

BAG OUTSIDE (WS)

LINING (WS)

14 Turn the bag right side out. Hand stitch the opening in the lining closed.

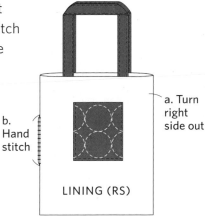

b. Hand stitch

a. Turn right side out

LINING (RS)

11½ in (29 cm)

9 in (23 cm)

how to stitch the circle tote bag

The following guide shows how to stitch a circle motif on a project that will be finished with a backing or lining.

1   Make a knot at the end of your thread and draw the needle out at the starting point at the 12 o'clock position of the first circle (☆). Stitch ¼ of the circle, stopping at the 9 o'clock position. Bring the needle to the 3 o'clock position on the next circle and stitch the lower half, stopping at the 9 o'clock position. Follow the same process to move to the next circle.

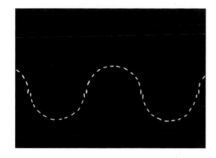
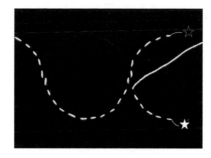

2 Follow the same process to stitch half of each circle in the row, alternating upper half and lower half each time. When you reach the end of the row, make a knot on the wrong side of the fabric.

3 Make a knot at the end of a new thread and draw the needle out at the starting point at the 6 o'clock position of the first circle (★). You'll follow the same process to stitch the remaining half of each circle in the first row.

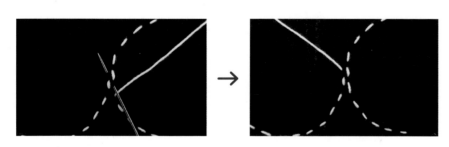
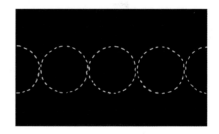

4 Note that for this project, the stitches should be slightly shifted where the circles meet.

5 Follow this process to finish stitching the first row of circles then make a knot when you reach the end. Repeat to stitch the remaining rows of circles.

· TIP ·

Adjacent circles look better when the stitches are shifted.

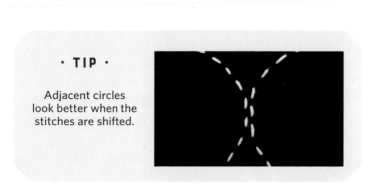

SASHIKO DIAGRAM

+ For best results, draw 2.75 cm grids. If you prefer to work in inches, draw 1 in grids, but please note that you may have to adjust the pattern as the resulting motif will have fewer repeats than pictured here.

+ For the pocket, align the center bottom of the template with the center bottom of the pocket and copy two rows of the pattern.

+ Stitch using a single strand of sashiko thread.

+ Refer to page 66 for stitching instructions. Follow the alphabetical order noted in the diagram.

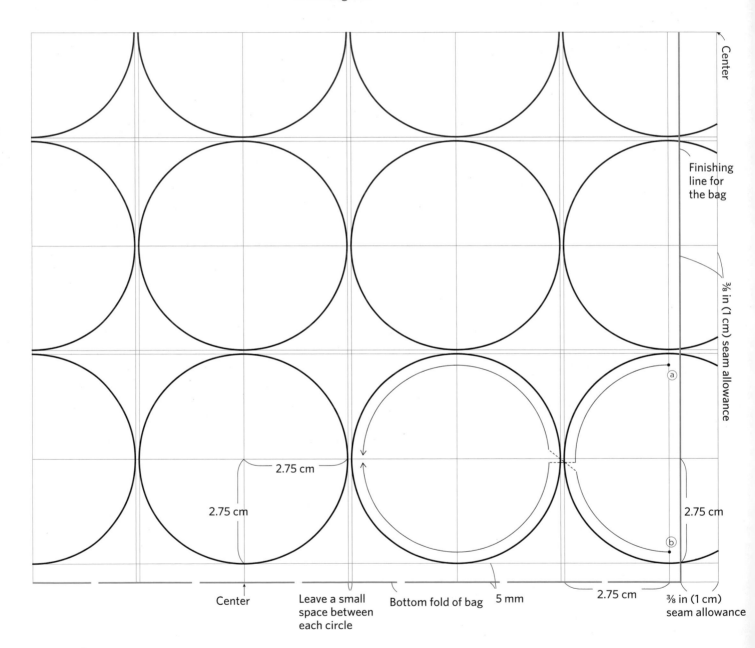

Center

Finishing line for the bag

³⁄₈ in (1 cm) seam allowance

ⓐ

ⓑ

2.75 cm

2.75 cm

2.75 cm

2.75 cm

Center

Leave a small space between each circle

Bottom fold of bag

5 mm

2.75 cm

³⁄₈ in (1 cm) seam allowance

COLORFUL CLASP PURSE

SHOWN ON PAGE 12

MATERIALS

+ OUTSIDE FABRIC: 12 in (30 cm) square of light purple linen
+ LINING FABRIC: 12 in (30 cm) square of blue linen
+ FUSIBLE FLEECE: 12 in (30 cm) square
+ One 7 × 3 in (18 × 7.5 cm) round glue in metal clasp
+ Sashiko thread in yellow, white, and gray
+ Craft glue

INSTRUCTIONS

1 Use the template on page 72 to cut one front and one back out of light purple linen. Mark 5 mm square grid lines on the front and stitch the motif as noted on page 72. Use the template to cut out two pieces of fusible fleece without seam allowance and adhere to the wrong side of the front and back.

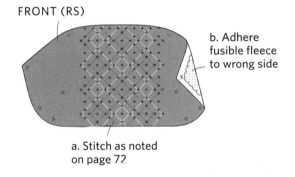

FRONT (RS)

b. Adhere fusible fleece to wrong side

a. Stitch as noted on page 72

2 Use the template to mark the dart placement, the sew the darts on both the front and back. Bring both thread tails to the wrong side and tie into a knot at the tip of the dart to secure. Trim the excess thread, leaving ⅜-¾ in (1-2 cm). Press the darts toward the outside.

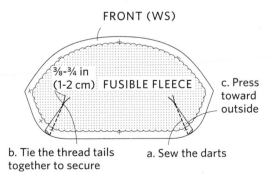

FRONT (WS)

⅜-¾ in (1-2 cm)   FUSIBLE FLEECE

c. Press toward outside

b. Tie the thread tails together to secure

a. Sew the darts

3 Align the front and back with right sides together and sew together along the bottom. Press the seam allowance open.

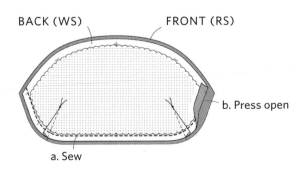

BACK (WS)   FRONT (RS)

b. Press open

a. Sew

4 Use the template on page 72 to cut two linings of blue linen. Follow the same process used in step 2 to sew the darts on both the front and back lining, but press the darts toward the center.

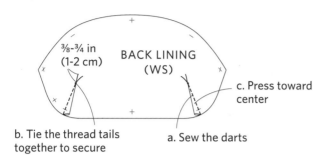

⅜-¾ in (1-2 cm)

BACK LINING (WS)

c. Press toward center

b. Tie the thread tails together to secure

a. Sew the darts

5 Align the front and back lining with right sides together and sew along the bottom. Press the seam allowance open.

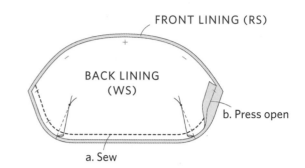

FRONT LINING (RS)

BACK LINING (WS)

b. Press open

a. Sew

6 Turn right side out. Insert the lining into the outside with right sides together. Sew together around the top, leaving a 3 in (8 cm) opening. Make clips into the curved sections of the seam allowance.

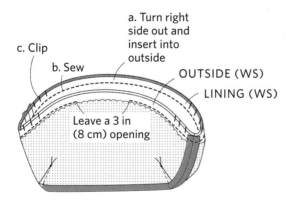

c. Clip

b. Sew

a. Turn right side out and insert into outside

OUTSIDE (WS)

LINING (WS)

Leave a 3 in (8 cm) opening

7 Turn right side out. Fold the opening seam allowances in and topstitch around the top, stitching close to the edge.

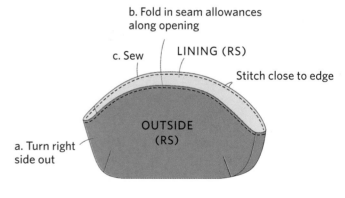

b. Fold in seam allowances along opening

c. Sew

LINING (RS)

Stitch close to edge

OUTSIDE (RS)

a. Turn right side out

8 Use a toothpick to apply glue to the channel on one half of the clasp. Use a screwdriver or stiletto to insert one half of the purse into the clasp. Next, cut the paper string in half to match the length of each side of the clasp. Insert a piece of paper string into the channel to help hold the fabric in place. Finally, use pliers and a scrap of batting to squeeze the clasp just above each hinge. Repeat process to install the other half of the clasp.

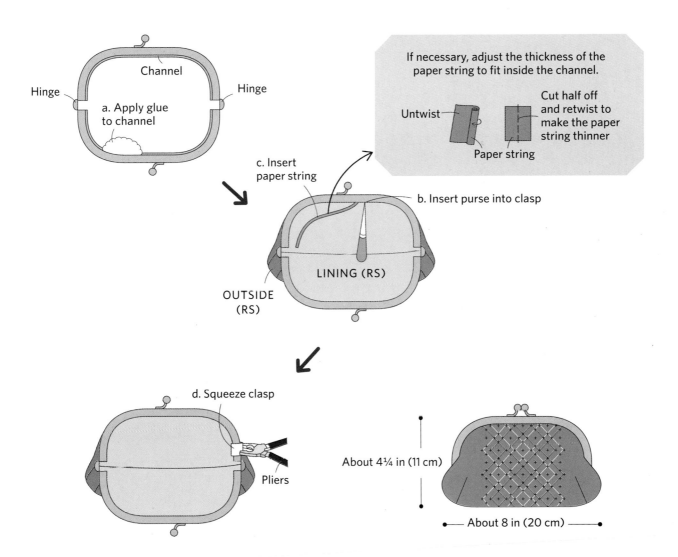

Channel

Hinge

Hinge

a. Apply glue to channel

If necessary, adjust the thickness of the paper string to fit inside the channel.

Untwist

Cut half off and retwist to make the paper string thinner

Paper string

c. Insert paper string

b. Insert purse into clasp

OUTSIDE (RS)

LINING (RS)

d. Squeeze clasp

Pliers

About 4¼ in (11 cm)

About 8 in (20 cm)

SASHIKO DIAGRAM & FULL SIZE TEMPLATE

+ For best results, draw 5 mm grids. If you prefer to work in inches, draw ¼ in grids, but please note that you may have to adjust the pattern as the resulting motif will have fewer repeats than pictured here.

+ Stitch using a single strand of sashiko thread.

+ The sashiko motif only appears on the front.

+ Stitch following the alphabetical order noted in the diagram.

PURSE

+ Cut 2 of outside fabric

+ Cut 2 of lining fabric

+ Cut 2 of fusible fleece (without seam allowance)

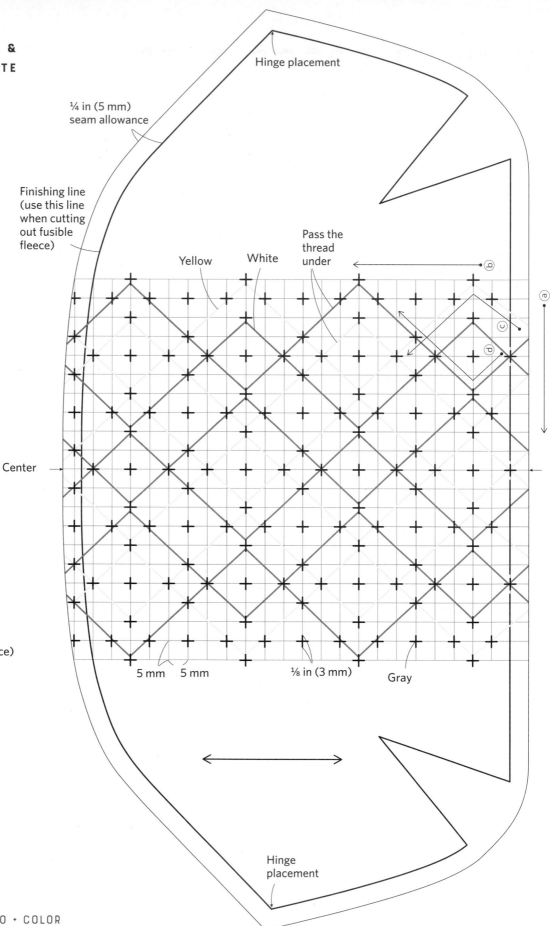

Hinge placement

¼ in (5 mm) seam allowance

Finishing line (use this line when cutting out fusible fleece)

Yellow

White

Pass the thread under

Center

5 mm 5 mm ⅛ in (3 mm) Gray

Hinge placement

FLOWER CROSS TOTE

SHOWN ON PAGE 14

MATERIALS

+ FRONT FABRIC: 12 in (30 cm) square of white linen
+ BACK AND HANDLE FABRIC: 20 × 12 in (50 × 30 cm) of navy linen
+ LINING FABRIC: 12 × 20 in (30 × 50 cm) of checkered cotton
+ Sashiko thread in navy

INSTRUCTIONS

1 Cut a 10¼ in (26 cm) square of white linen for the front. Mark 5 mm grid lines on the fabric in the area noted below.

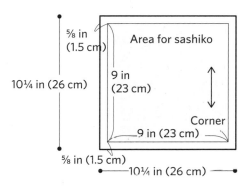

2 Stitch the motif as noted on page 77. Mark the finishing lines following the dimensions noted below. Trim into a 9½ in (24 cm) square.

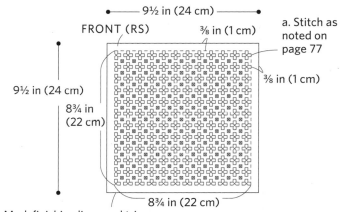

b. Mark finishing lines and trim

3 Cut a 9½ in (24 cm) square of navy linen for the back. Align the front and back with right sides together and sew along the sides and bottom using ⅜ in (1 cm) seam allowance. Trim the bottom corner seam allowances at an angle. Press all seam allowances open.

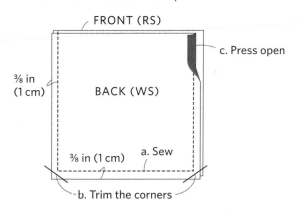

4 Cut a 9½ × 18¼ in (24 × 46 cm) rectangle of checkered cotton for the lining. Fold in half with right sides together. Sew together along the sides using ⅜ in (1 cm) seam allowance. Leave a 3 in (8 cm) opening in one of the sides. Press the seam allowances open.

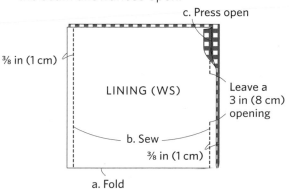

5 Cut two 5½ × 11 in (13 × 28 cm) rectangles of navy linen for the handles. Fold each handle in half with right sides together. Sew along the long side using ⅜ in (1 cm) seam allowance. Turn right side out.

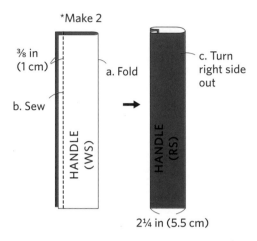

*Make 2

⅜ in (1 cm)

b. Sew

a. Fold

c. Turn right side out

HANDLE (WS)

HANDLE (RS)

2¼ in (5.5 cm)

6 Turn the bag right side out. Align the seams of the handles with the side seams of the bag. Temporarily baste in place as shown below.

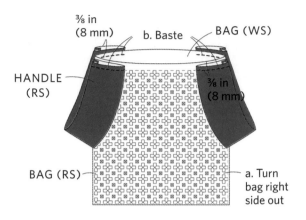

⅜ in (8 mm)

b. Baste

BAG (WS)

HANDLE (RS)

⅜ in (8 mm)

BAG (RS)

a. Turn bag right side out

7 Insert the bag into the lining with right sides together. Sew together around the bag opening.

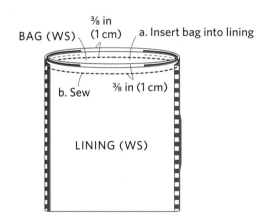

BAG (WS)

⅜ in (1 cm)

a. Insert bag into lining

b. Sew

⅜ in (1 cm)

LINING (WS)

8 Turn right side out. Fold the seam allowances in and hand stitch the opening in the lining closed.

a. Turn right side out

b. Hand stitch

LINING (RS)

13¾ in (35 cm)

8¾ in (22 cm)

8¾ in (22 cm)

FLOWER CROSS ZIP POUCH

✎ SHOWN ON PAGE 14

MATERIALS

+ OUTSIDE FABRIC: 8 × 12 in (20 × 30 cm) of white linen
+ LINING FABRIC: 8 × 10 in (20 × 25 cm) of checkered cotton
+ One 5 in (14 cm) zipper
+ Sashiko thread in navy

INSTRUCTIONS

1 Cut a 7½ × 10¾ in (19 × 27 cm) rectangle of white linen for the pouch outside. Mark 5 mm grid lines on the fabric in the area noted below.

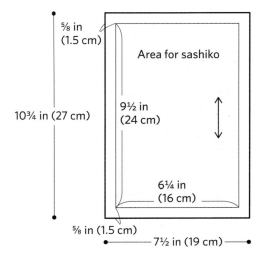

⅝ in (1.5 cm)

Area for sashiko

10¾ in (27 cm)

9½ in (24 cm)

6¼ in (16 cm)

⅝ in (1.5 cm)

7½ in (19 cm)

2 Stitch the motif as noted on page 77. Mark the finishing lines following the dimensions noted below. Trim into a 6¾ × 9¾ in (17 × 25 cm) rectangle, keeping the sashiko design centered.

3 Align the right side of the zipper with the pouch outside, so the zipper is positioned ¼ in (5 mm) from the top edge. Fold the ends of the zipper into triangles as shown and baste the zipper in place.

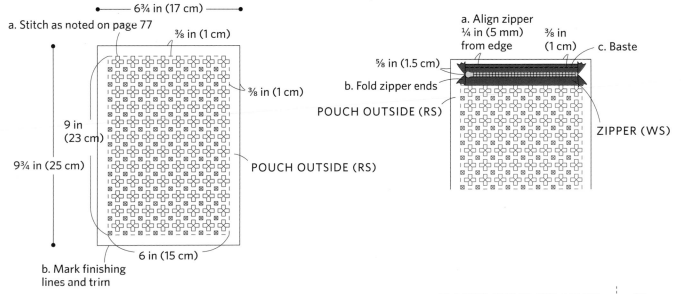

6¾ in (17 cm)

a. Stitch as noted on page 77

⅜ in (1 cm)

⅜ in (1 cm)

9 in (23 cm)

9¾ in (25 cm)

POUCH OUTSIDE (RS)

6 in (15 cm)

b. Mark finishing lines and trim

a. Align zipper ¼ in (5 mm) from edge

⅜ in (1 cm)

c. Baste

⅝ in (1.5 cm)

b. Fold zipper ends

POUCH OUTSIDE (RS)

ZIPPER (WS)

4 Cut a 6¾ × 9¾ in (17 × 25 cm) rectangle of checkered cotton for the lining. Align the lining and pouch outside with right sides together. Sew together along the top, stitching ½ in (1.2 cm) from the edge.

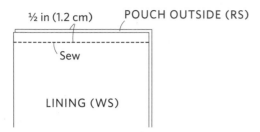

½ in (1.2 cm)   POUCH OUTSIDE (RS)

Sew

LINING (WS)

5 Turn right side out and adjust so that the lining is on the inside.

ZIPPER (RS)

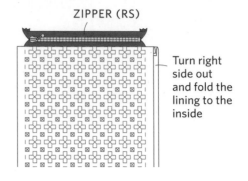

Turn right side out and fold the lining to the inside

6 Fold the bottom edge of the pouch outside so it extends ¼ in (5 mm) beyond the edge of the zipper. Baste the zipper in place, stitching ⅜ in (1 cm) from the edge of the fabric.

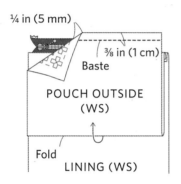

¼ in (5 mm)

⅜ in (1 cm)

Baste

POUCH OUTSIDE (WS)

Fold

LINING (WS)

7 Next, fold the bottom edge of the lining so it matches up with the pouch outside along the top. Make sure to fold it with right sides together so it is the bottom layer. Sew along the top to secure everything in place, stitching ½ in (1.2 cm) from the edge of the fabric.

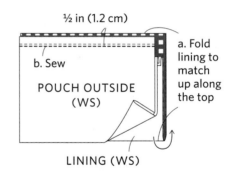

½ in (1.2 cm)

b. Sew

POUCH OUTSIDE (WS)

a. Fold lining to match up along the top

LINING (WS)

8 Open the pouch so that the seam from step 7 is centered and the two halves of the lining are positioned on one side and the two halves of the pouch outside are positioned on the other. Sew together along the sides using ⅜ in (1 cm) seam allowance and leave a 2¾ in (7 cm) opening in one side of the lining.

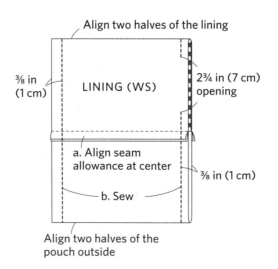

Align two halves of the lining

⅜ in (1 cm)

LINING (WS)

2¾ in (7 cm) opening

a. Align seam allowance at center

⅜ in (1 cm)

b. Sew

Align two halves of the pouch outside

9 Turn right side out. Fold the seam allowances in and hand stitch the opening in the lining closed.

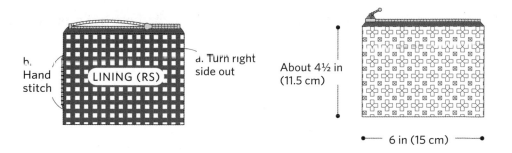

h. Hand stitch

d. Turn right side out

LINING (RS)

About 4½ in (11.5 cm)

6 in (15 cm)

SASHIKO DIAGRAM

+ For best results, draw 5 mm grids. If you prefer to work in inches, draw ¼ in grids, but please note that you may have to adjust the pattern as the resulting motif will have fewer repeats than pictured here.

+ Stitch using a single strand of sashiko thread.

+ Stitch following the alphabetical order noted in the diagram.

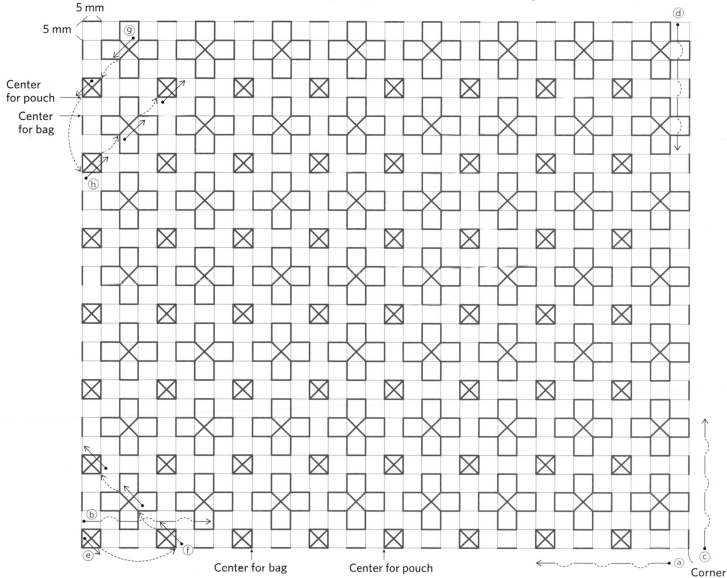

5 mm

5 mm

Center for pouch

Center for bag

Center for bag

Center for pouch

Corner

BOXY POUCH

SHOWN ON PAGE 16

MATERIALS

+ OUTSIDE FABRIC: 12 × 14 in (30 × 35 cm) of red linen
+ LINING FABRIC: 12 × 14 in (30 × 35 cm) of dark pink linen
+ One 8 in (20 cm) zipper
+ Sashiko thread in white

INSTRUCTIONS

1 Cut a 9¼ × 14 in (23 × 35 cm) rectangle of red linen for the pouch outside. Mark 5 mm grid lines on the fabric in the area noted below.

2 Stitch the motif as noted on page 81. Mark the finishing lines following the dimensions noted below. Trim into an 8¾ × 13½ in (22 × 34 cm) rectangle, keeping the sashiko design centered. Take care not to cut through the stitching.

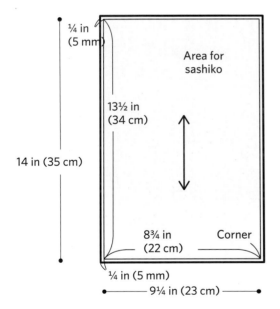

¼ in (5 mm)

Area for sashiko

13½ in (34 cm)

14 in (35 cm)

8¾ in (22 cm)   Corner

¼ in (5 mm)

9¼ in (23 cm)

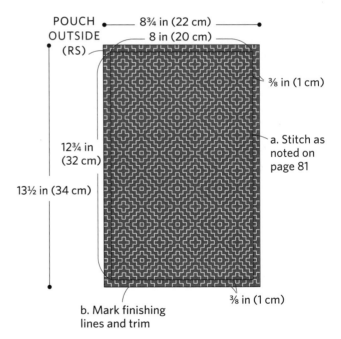

POUCH OUTSIDE (RS)

8¾ in (22 cm)

8 in (20 cm)

⅜ in (1 cm)

12¾ in (32 cm)

13½ in (34 cm)

a. Stitch as noted on page 81

b. Mark finishing lines and trim

⅜ in (1 cm)

3 Fold and press the top edge over ⅜ in (1 cm) to the wrong side. Align the folded edge ⅜ in (1 cm) from the center of the zipper and topstitch, stitching as close to the fold as possible. Follow the same process to attach the bottom edge to the other side of the zipper.

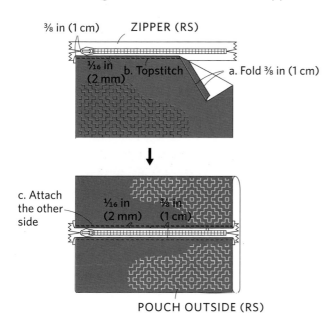

⅜ in (1 cm) ZIPPER (RS)

1/16 in (2 mm) b. Topstitch a. Fold ⅜ in (1 cm)

c. Attach the other side

1/16 in (2 mm) ⅜ in (1 cm)

POUCH OUTSIDE (RS)

4 Cut two 2¾ in (7 cm) squares of red linen for the tabs. Fold and press the top and bottom edges over ⅜ in (1 cm) to the wrong side. Next, fold each tab in half lengthwise and topstitch along the top and bottom, stitching as close to the edges as possible. Finally, fold each tab in half widthwise and baste together ⅜ in (1 cm) from the edge.

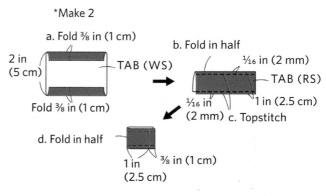

*Make 2

a. Fold ⅜ in (1 cm)

b. Fold in half

2 in (5 cm) TAB (WS) 1/16 in (2 mm)

Fold ⅜ in (1 cm) TAB (RS)

1/16 in (2 mm) c. Topstitch 1 in (2.5 cm)

d. Fold in half

1 in (2.5 cm) ⅜ in (1 cm)

5 Turn the pouch outside inside out so the wrong side is facing up. Cut an 8¾ × 13½ in (22 × 34 cm) rectangle of dark pink linen for the lining. Fold and press the top and bottom edges of the lining over ⅜ in (1 cm) to the wrong side. Wrap the lining around the pouch outside with wrong sides together and hand stitch the folded edges of the lining to the zipper tape.

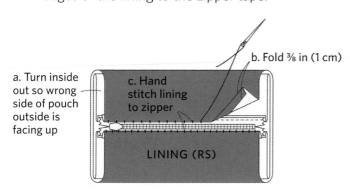

a. Turn inside out so wrong side of pouch outside is facing up

b. Fold ⅜ in (1 cm)

c. Hand stitch lining to zipper

LINING (RS)

6 To create the box, tuck and fold the top and bottom edges in to the center. You'll have two separate layers as shown in the diagram. Sandwich the tabs between the layers, aligning the center of the tab with the center of the zipper tape on each end of the pouch.

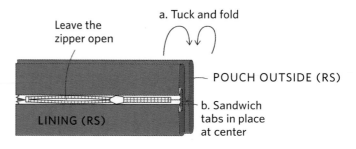

Leave the zipper open

a. Tuck and fold

POUCH OUTSIDE (RS)

LINING (RS)

b. Sandwich tabs in place at center

7 Sew all the layers together along the sides using ⅜ in (1 cm) seam allowance. Make sure to leave the zipper partially open. Note: The side seams should be about 3 in (8 cm) long.

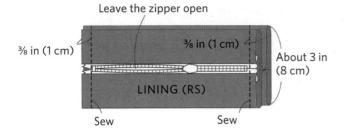

Leave the zipper open

⅜ in (1 cm)

⅜ in (1 cm)

About 3 in (8 cm)

LINING (RS)

Sew   Sew

8 Cut two 1¾ × 4¼ in (4.5 × 10.5 cm) rectangles of dark pink linen to bind the seam allowances. Fold and press the top and bottom edges over ⅜ in (1 cm) to the wrong side. Next, fold and press the left and right edges over ⅜ in (1 cm) to the wrong side. Finally, fold each piece in half widthwise.

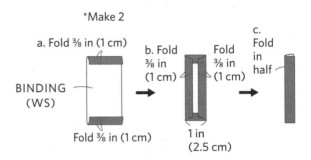

*Make 2

a. Fold ⅜ in (1 cm)

b. Fold ⅜ in (1 cm)   Fold ⅜ in (1 cm)

c. Fold in half

BINDING (WS)

Fold ⅜ in (1 cm)

1 in (2.5 cm)

9 Wrap the bindings around the side seam allowances and hand stitch in place. Again, make sure the zipper is open.

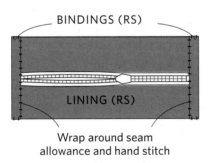

BINDINGS (RS)

LINING (RS)

Wrap around seam allowance and hand stitch

10 Turn the pouch right side out and adjust the shape.

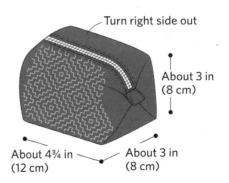

Turn right side out

About 3 in (8 cm)

About 4¾ in (12 cm)

About 3 in (8 cm)

SASHIKO DIAGRAM

+ For best results, draw 5 mm grids. If you prefer to work in inches, draw ¼ in grids, but please note that you may have to adjust the pattern as the resulting motif will have fewer repeats than pictured here.

+ Stitch using a single strand of sashiko thread.

+ Stitch following the alphabetical order noted in the diagram.

DOT PATTERN TOTE BAG

SHOWN ON PAGE 17

MATERIALS

+ OUTSIDE FABRIC: 20 × 31½ in (50 × 80 cm) of navy cotton
+ LINING FABRIC: 24 × 20 in (60 × 50 cm) of striped cotton
+ BATTING: 24 × 24 in (60 × 60 cm)
+ FUSIBLE INTERFACING: 16 × 24 in (40 × 60 cm)
+ CARD STOCK: 2¾ × 10¾ in (7 × 27 cm)
+ Sashiko thread in off-white

INSTRUCTIONS

1 Cut a 14¼ × 17½ in (36 × 45 cm) rectangle of navy cotton for the bag outside. Mark the finishing lines ⅜ in (1 cm) in from each edge and mark the center. Starting at the center, mark vertical lines spaced ⅝ in (1.5 cm) apart. Stitch the motif as noted on page 87 (also refer to page 86). Note: Do not stitch the fourth lines in the sashiko motif at this point—you'll finish these in step 3.

2 Cut two 14¼ × 2½ in (36 × 6 cm) rectangles of navy cotton for the outside facings. With right sides together, sew the outside facings to the top and bottom edges of the bag outside using ⅜ in (1 cm) seam allowance. Press the seam allowances toward the facings.

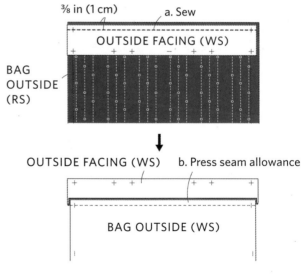

⅜ in (1 cm)   a. Sew

OUTSIDE FACING (WS)

BAG OUTSIDE (RS)

OUTSIDE FACING (WS)   b. Press seam allowance

BAG OUTSIDE (WS)

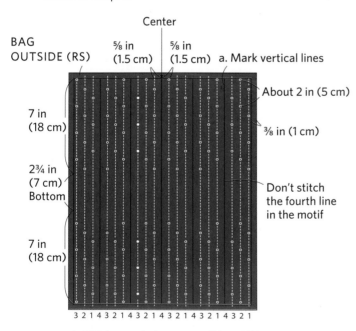

Center

BAG OUTSIDE (RS)

⅝ in (1.5 cm)   ⅝ in (1.5 cm)   a. Mark vertical lines

About 2 in (5 cm)

⅜ in (1 cm)

7 in (18 cm)

2¾ in (7 cm) Bottom

Don't stitch the fourth line in the motif

7 in (18 cm)

3 2 1 4 3 2 1 4 3 2 1 4 3 2 1 4 3 2 1 4 3 2 1

b. Stitch as noted on pages 86 and 87

*Don't make French knots along the bottom

3 Cut a 14¼ × 21½ in (36 × 53 cm) piece of batting and align on the wrong side of the assembled bag outside. Baste together around all four sides. Complete the embroidery on the fourth lines of the sashiko motif omitted in step 1. Remove the basting stitches and adhere a 14¼ × 21½ in (36 × 53 cm) piece of fusible interfacing to the batting.

4 Fold in half with right sides together. Sew together along the sides using ⅜ in (1 cm) seam allowance. Press the seams open.

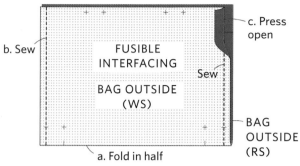

b. Sew
FUSIBLE INTERFACING
BAG OUTSIDE (WS)
Sew
c. Press open
a. Fold in half
BAG OUTSIDE (RS)

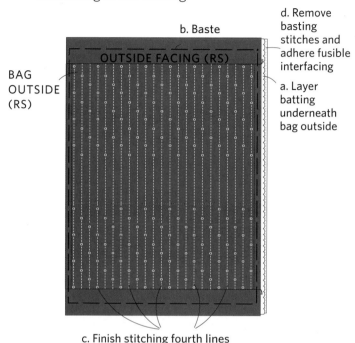

BAG OUTSIDE (RS)

b. Baste
OUTSIDE FACING (RS)

d. Remove basting stitches and adhere fusible interfacing

a. Layer batting underneath bag outside

c. Finish stitching fourth lines

5 Cut a 6 × 8¾ in (15 × 22 cm) rectangle of striped cotton for the pocket. Fold in half with right sides together. Sew together around three sides using ⅜ in (1 cm) seam allowance. Make sure to leave a 2 in (5 cm) opening along the bottom. Trim the corner seam allowances at an angle. Turn right side out. Fold the opening seam allowances in and hand stitch closed. Topstitch the top edge of the pocket.

6 Cut a 14¼ × 17½ in (36 × 45 cm) rectangle of striped cotton for the bag lining. Topstitch the pocket to the lining following the placement noted below.

LINING (RS)
4½ in (11.5 cm)
POCKET (RS)
1¼ in (3 cm)
Topstitch
1/16 in (2 mm)

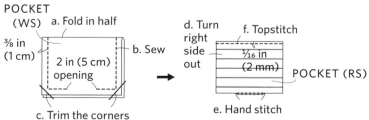

POCKET (WS)
⅜ in (1 cm)
a. Fold in half
2 in (5 cm) opening
b. Sew
c. Trim the corners
d. Turn right side out
f. Topstitch
1/16 in (2 mm)
POCKET (RS)
e. Hand stitch

7 Cut two 14¼ × 2¼ in (36 × 6 cm) rectangles of navy cotton for the inside facings. With right sides together, sew the inside facings to the top and bottom edges of the lining using ⅜ in (1 cm) seam allowance. Press the seam allowances toward the facings. Topstitch the facings, stitching as close to the seam as possible.

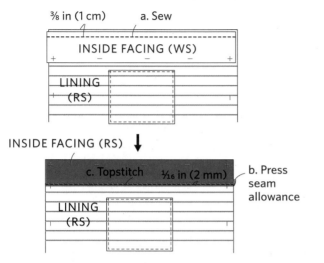

⅜ in (1 cm)   a. Sew

INSIDE FACING (WS)

LINING (RS)

INSIDE FACING (RS)

c. Topstitch   ¹⁄₁₆ in (2 mm)   b. Press seam allowance

LINING (RS)

8 Fold the assembled lining in half with right sides together. Sew together along the sides using ⅜ in (1 cm) seam allowance. Press the seams open.

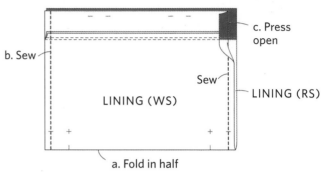

b. Sew

c. Press open

Sew

LINING (WS)   LINING (RS)

a. Fold in half

9 Miter the corners on both the bag outside and lining: Align each side seam with the bottom fold of the bag to create a triangular corner. Sew across the base of each triangle with a 2¾ in (7 cm) long seam. Press the seam allowances up.

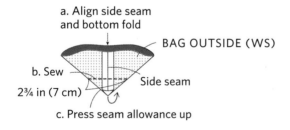

a. Align side seam and bottom fold

BAG OUTSIDE (WS)

b. Sew

2¾ in (7 cm)   Side seam

c. Press seam allowance up

10 Cut two 3½ × 12¾ in (9 × 32 cm) rectangles of navy cotton and two of batting. Fold each fabric rectangle in half widthwise with right sides together. Fold each batting rectangle in half widthwise and align on top. Sew together along one long edge. Trim the excess batting from the seam allowance. Turn the handles right side out and align the seams at the center. Finally, running stitch beside the seam using two strands of sashiko thread.

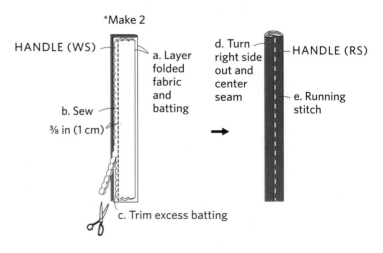

*Make 2

HANDLE (WS)

a. Layer folded fabric and batting

b. Sew

⅜ in (1 cm)

c. Trim excess batting

d. Turn right side out and center seam

HANDLE (RS)

e. Running stitch

11 Turn the bag outside right side out. Baste the handles to the outside facings following the placement noted at right. Cut a 2¾ × 10¾ in (7 × 27 cm) rectangle of card stock for the bottom and insert into the bag.

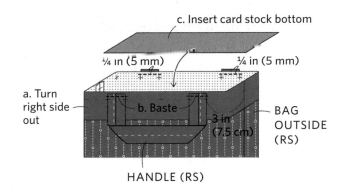

c. Insert card stock bottom

¼ in (5 mm) ¼ in (5 mm)

a. Turn right side out

b. Baste

3 in (7.5 cm)

BAG OUTSIDE (RS)

HANDLE (RS)

12 Fold and press the top edge of the facings over ⅜ in (1 cm) to the wrong side on both the bag outside and lining. Insert the lining into the bag outside with wrong sides together.

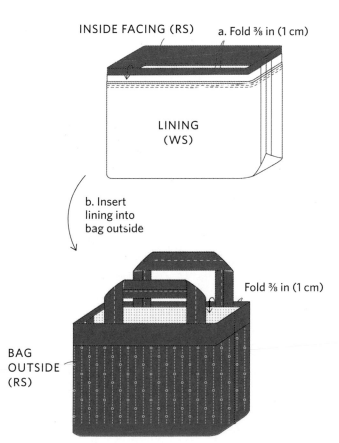

INSIDE FACING (RS)   a. Fold ⅜ in (1 cm)

LINING (WS)

b. Insert lining into bag outside

Fold ⅜ in (1 cm)

BAG OUTSIDE (RS)

13 Topstitch around the top of the bag, stitching ⅛ in (4 mm) from the edge.

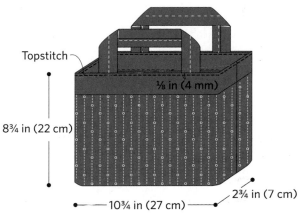

Topstitch

⅛ in (4 mm)

8¾ in (22 cm)

10¾ in (27 cm)

2¾ in (7 cm)

how to stitch the dot pattern tote bag

This design incorporates French knots to accent the vertical lines of running stitch.

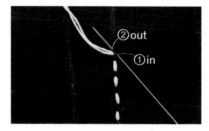

1 Use two strands of sashiko thread to make 8-9 running stitches (each stitch should be about ⅛ in [3 mm] long). Draw the needle out and make a small diagonal stitch to anchor the thread. Do not pull the needle through the fabric.

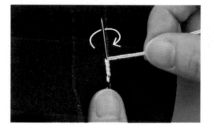

2 Wrap the thread around the needle four times.

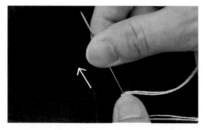

3 Use your thumb to hold the wrapped thread in place against the fabric. Pull the needle through the wraps.

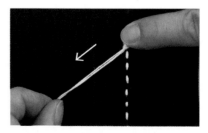

4 Use your index finger to hold the knot in place against the fabric and adjust the shape while pulling the thread.

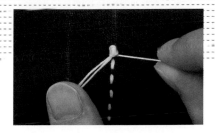

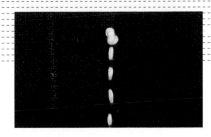

5 Insert the needle back through the fabric right next to the knot.

6 Completed view of the French knot.

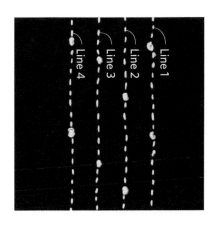

Line 4 Line 3 Line 2 Line 1

7 Continue stitching the vertical line, making French knots every 8-9 stitches. Do not make French knots along the bottom portion of the bag—this area will be running stitch only. When stitching the second and third lines, stagger the French knots as shown at left. The fourth line will be completed after you begin construction the bag, but the French knots in the fourth line should align with those in the first line.

SASHIKO DIAGRAM

+ Stitch using two strands of sashiko thread.

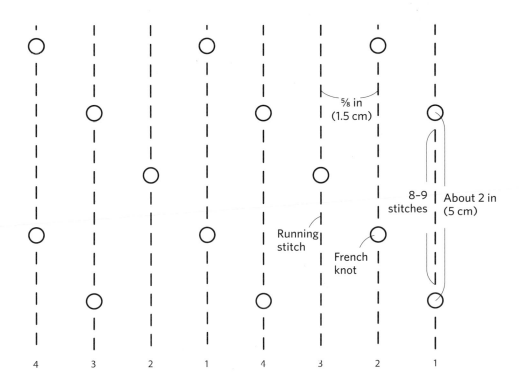

⅝ in (1.5 cm)

8-9 stitches

About 2 in (5 cm)

Running stitch

French knot

4 3 2 1 4 3 2 1

BISCORNU PIN CUSHIONS

SHOWN ON PAGE 18

MATERIALS

FOR A

+ FABRIC A: 4 in (10 cm) square of white linen
+ FABRIC B: 4 in (10 cm) square of magenta linen
+ BUTTONS: Two ⅜ in (8 mm) diameter
+ About 10 g of cotton stuffing
+ Fine sashiko thread in teal and mint

FOR B

+ FABRIC A: 4 in (10 cm) square of white linen
+ FABRIC B: 4 in (10 cm) square of vermilion linen
+ BUTTONS: Two ⅜ in (8 mm) diameter
+ About 10 g of cotton stuffing
+ Fine sashiko thread in vermilion and yellow

INSTRUCTIONS

1 Mark 5 mm square grid lines on fabric A and stitch the motif as noted on page 90. Align fabrics A and B with right sides together so the top left corner of A matches up with the top center point of B. Sew from ♡ to △.

2 Flip the work over so the right side of A is facing up. Make a clip into the corner seam allowance of B only, stopping at the △. Next, align fabrics A and B with right sides together so the top right corner of B matches up with the right center point of A. Sew from △ to ♡.

Align top left corner of A with top center point of B

Align top center point of A with top right corner of B

FABRIC B (RS)

b. Sew

a. Stitch right side as noted on page 90

FABRIC A (WS)

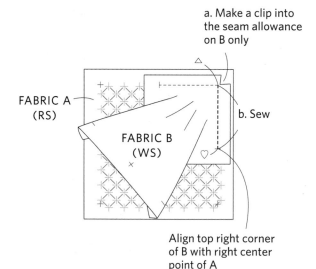

a. Make a clip into the seam allowance on B only

FABRIC A (RS)

b. Sew

FABRIC B (WS)

Align top right corner of B with right center point of A

3 Follow the same process used in steps 1 and 2 to sew the pin cushion together, leaving one side open. Remember to make clips into the seam allowances at the △s to help align the center points of one fabric with the corners of the other.

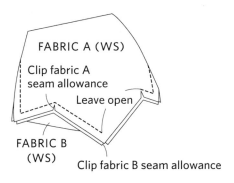

FABRIC A (WS)

Clip fabric A seam allowance

Leave open

FABRIC B (WS)

Clip fabric B seam allowance

4 Turn the pin cushion right side out. Insert the stuffing and hand stitch the remaining side closed. Blanket stitch along the seam line dividing the top and bottom of the pin cushion, as shown below.

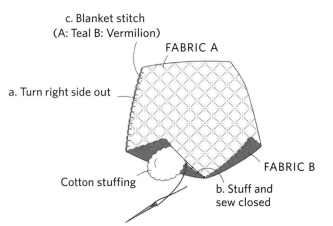

c. Blanket stitch
(A: Teal B: Vermilion)

FABRIC A

a. Turn right side out

Cotton stuffing

FABRIC B

b. Stuff and sew closed

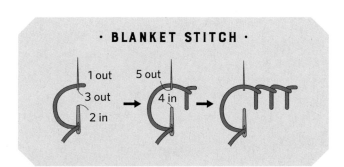

· BLANKET STITCH ·

1 out
3 out
2 in
→
5 out
4 in
→

5 Use a single thread to sew one button to the center of the top and one button to the center of the bottom. Pull the thread taut to make an indent at the center of the pin cushion, then knot to secure.

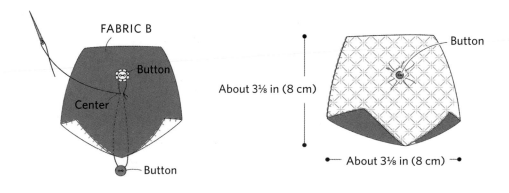

FABRIC B

Button

Center

Button

Button

About 3⅛ in (8 cm)

About 3⅛ in (8 cm)

SASHIKO DIAGRAM

+ For best results, draw 5 mm grids. If you prefer to work in inches, draw ¼ in grids, but please note that you may have to adjust the pattern as the resulting motif will have fewer repeats than pictured here.

+ Stitch using a single strand of sashiko thread.

+ Stitch following the alphabetical order noted in the diagram.

☆ = Center

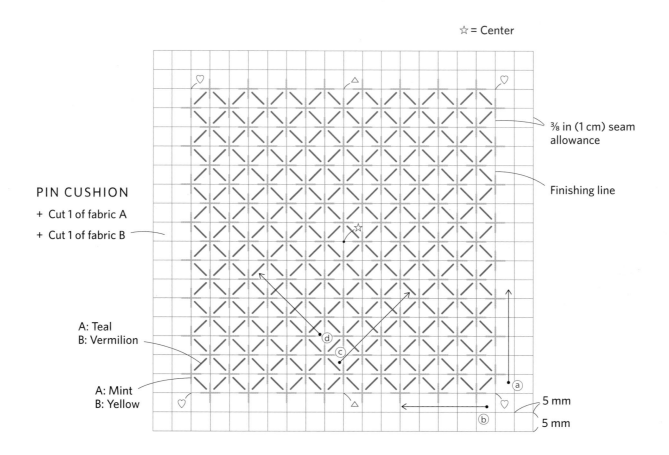

⅜ in (1 cm) seam allowance

Finishing line

PIN CUSHION

+ Cut 1 of fabric A

+ Cut 1 of fabric B

A: Teal
B: Vermilion

A: Mint
B: Yellow

5 mm

5 mm

BUTTON BROOCHES

SHOWN ON PAGE 19

SHOWN ON PAGE 19

MATERIALS

FOR ONE BROOCH

+ MAIN FABRIC: 4 in (10 cm) square of white cotton

+ FELT: 2½ in (6 cm) square of gray felt

+ One 1½ in (3.8 cm) diameter cover button set (preferably shankless)

+ One 1 in (2.5 cm) brooch pin

+ Fine sashiko thread in vermilion (for A), emerald (for B), or black (for C)

INSTRUCTIONS

1 Mark square grid lines on the main fabric (refer to individual template for dimensions) and stitch the motif as noted on page 92. Once the stitching is complete, use the template to cut the brooch into shape.

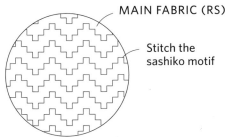

MAIN FABRIC (RS)

Stitch the sashiko motif

2 Align the embroidered fabric on top of the cover button holder with the wrong side facing up. Align the cover button on top with the hollow side facing up. Use the tool to press down so the fabric wraps around the cover button. Next, align the backing on top and use the tool to firmly insert the backing. Remove the completed covered button from the holder.

3 Use the template on page 92 to cut a circle out of felt to match the size of the cover button backing. Sew a brooch pin to the felt following the placement noted below. Glue the felt to the cover button backing. Use the template on page 92 to cut a rectangle out of felt and glue on top of the brooch pin to prevent it from snagging on clothes.

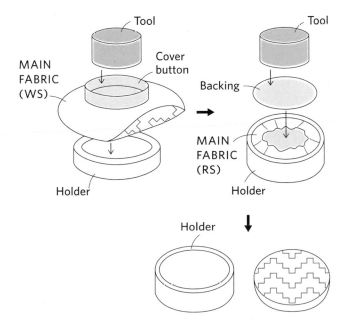

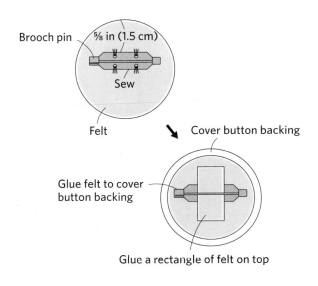

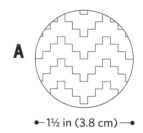

A

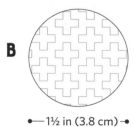

B

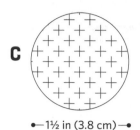

C

●—1½ in (3.8 cm)—●   ●—1½ in (3.8 cm)—●   ●—1½ in (3.8 cm)—●

SASHIKO DIAGRAMS & FULL SIZE TEMPLATES

+ For best results, draw either 3 or 4 mm grids as noted on the templates below. If you prefer to work in inches, draw ⅛ in grids, but please note that you may have to adjust the pattern as the resulting motif will have fewer repeats than pictured here.

+ Stitch using a single strand of sashiko thread.

+ Stitch following the alphabetical order noted on the templates.

+ Use the sashiko templates to trim the fabric into shape in step 1.

A

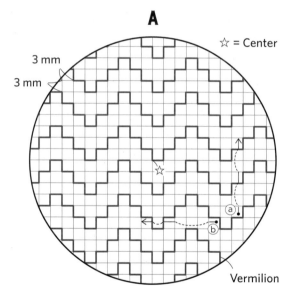

☆ = Center

3 mm

3 mm

ⓐ
ⓑ

Vermilion

B

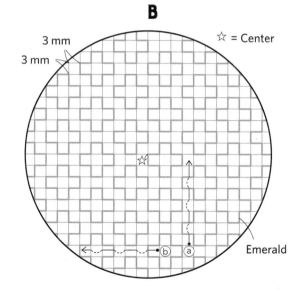

☆ = Center

3 mm

3 mm

ⓑ ⓐ

Emerald

C

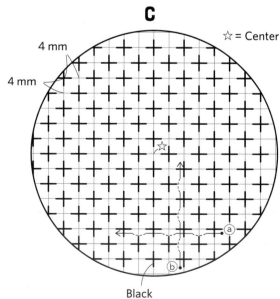

☆ = Center

4 mm

4 mm

ⓐ
ⓑ

Black

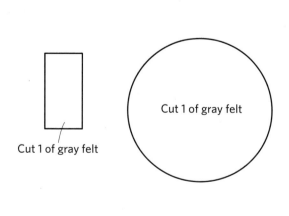

Cut 1 of gray felt

Cut 1 of gray felt

DRAWSTRING POUCH

SHOWN ON PAGE 13

MATERIALS

+ OUTSIDE FABRIC: 16 × 10 in (40 × 25 cm) of white linen
+ LINING FABRIC: 8 × 18 in (20 × 45 cm) of pink linen
+ ROUND CORD: 40 in (100 cm) of ⅛ in (3 mm) diameter cord
+ Sashiko thread in light pink and light green

INSTRUCTIONS

1 Cut a 7½ × 8½ in (19 × 21.5 cm) rectangle of white linen for the front. Mark 5 mm grid lines on the fabric in the area noted below.

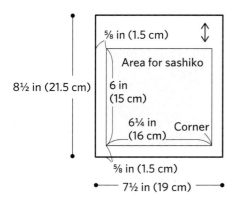

2 Stitch the motif as noted on page 97 (also refer to page 96). Mark the finishing lines following the dimensions noted below. Trim into a 6¾ × 7¾ in (17 × 20 cm) rectangle, keeping the sashiko design centered.

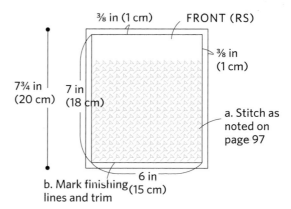

3 Cut another 6¾ × 7¾ in (17 × 20 cm) rectangle of white linen for the back. Fold and press the top edge over ⅜ in (1 cm) to the wrong side on both the front and back.

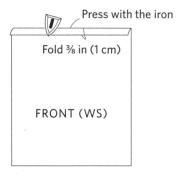

Press with the iron

Fold ⅜ in (1 cm)

FRONT (WS)

4 Unfold the top edges pressed in step 3. Align the front and back with right sides together. Sew together along the sides and bottom using ⅜ in (1 cm) seam allowance. Trim the bottom corner seam allowances at an angle. Press the side and bottom seam allowances open.

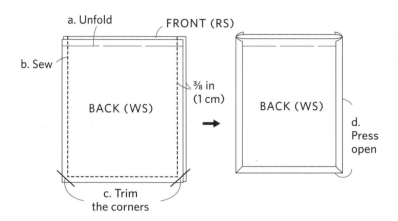

a. Unfold

FRONT (RS)

b. Sew

BACK (WS)

⅜ in (1 cm)

BACK (WS)

d. Press open

c. Trim the corners

5 Cut a 6¾ × 17¾ in (17 × 45 cm) rectangle of pink linen for the lining. Fold and press the top and bottom edges over 1¼ in (3 cm) to the wrong side.

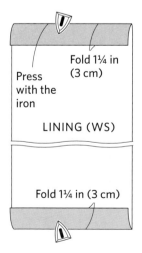

Fold 1¼ in (3 cm)

Press with the iron

LINING (WS)

Fold 1¼ in (3 cm)

6 Unfold the top and bottom edges pressed in step 5. Fold the lining in half with right sides together. Sew together along the sides using ⅜ in (1 cm) seam allowance, making sure to start or stop sewing 1¾ in (4.5 cm) from the top on both sides. This area will become the drawstring casing. Press the side seam allowances open.

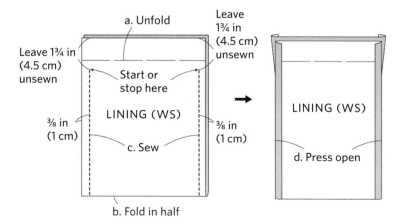

a. Unfold

Leave 1¾ in (4.5 cm) unsewn

Leave 1¾ in (4.5 cm) unsewn

Start or stop here

⅜ in (1 cm)

LINING (WS)

⅜ in (1 cm)

c. Sew

b. Fold in half

LINING (WS)

d. Press open

7 Next, you'll finish the edges for the drawstring casing on the lining. Fold and press the remaining raw edges over ¼ in (5 mm) twice. This is the area that was left unsewn in step 6. Topstitch in place by stitching in a V shape.

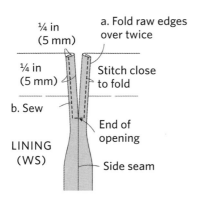

¼ in (5 mm)

a. Fold raw edges over twice

¼ in (5 mm)

Stitch close to fold

b. Sew

LINING (WS)

End of opening

Side seam

8 Turn the pouch right side out. Fold and press the top edges over ⅜ in (1 cm) to the wrong side along the creases made in step 3. On the lining, fold and press the top edges over 1¼ in (3 cm) to the wrong side along the creases made in step 5. Insert the lining into the pouch outside with wrong sides together.

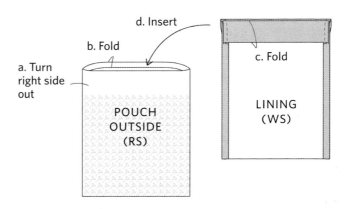

d. Insert

b. Fold

a. Turn right side out

c. Fold

POUCH OUTSIDE (RS)

LINING (WS)

9 The lining will extend ⅝ in (1.5 cm) above the pouch outside at the top. Topstitch around the pouch opening, stitching 1⁄16 in (2 mm) below where the pouch outside overlaps the lining.

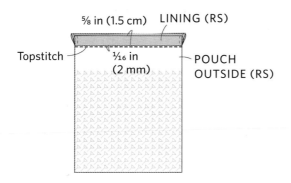

⅝ in (1.5 cm)   LINING (RS)

Topstitch

1⁄16 in (2 mm)

POUCH OUTSIDE (RS)

10 Cut two 20 in (50 cm) long pieces of cord. Insert each piece through the drawstring casing in opposite directions and tie the ends into a knot.

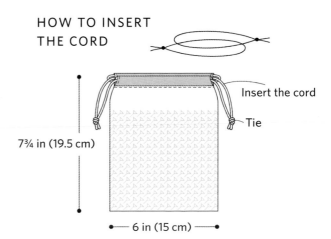

HOW TO INSERT THE CORD

Insert the cord

Tie

7¾ in (19.5 cm)

6 in (15 cm)

how to stitch the drawstring pouch

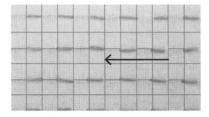

1 Start by stitching the horizontal rows (ⓐ and ⓑ) using a single strand of light pink sashiko thread.

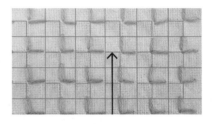

2 Next, stitch the vertical rows (ⓒ and ⓓ) using light pink sashiko thread.

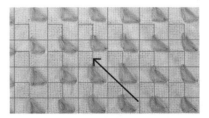

3 Stitch the left diagonal rows (ⓔ and ⓕ) using light pink sashiko thread.

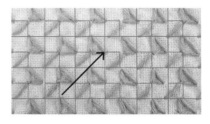

4 Finally, stitch the right diagonal rows (ⓖ and ⓗ) using a single strand of light green sashiko thread to create the stems.

SASHIKO DIAGRAM

+ For best results, draw 5 mm grids. If you prefer to work in inches, draw ¼ in grids, but please note that you may have to adjust the pattern as the resulting motif will have fewer repeats than pictured here.

+ Stitch using a single strand of sashiko thread.

+ Refer to page 96 for stitching instructions. Follow the alphabetical order noted in the diagram.

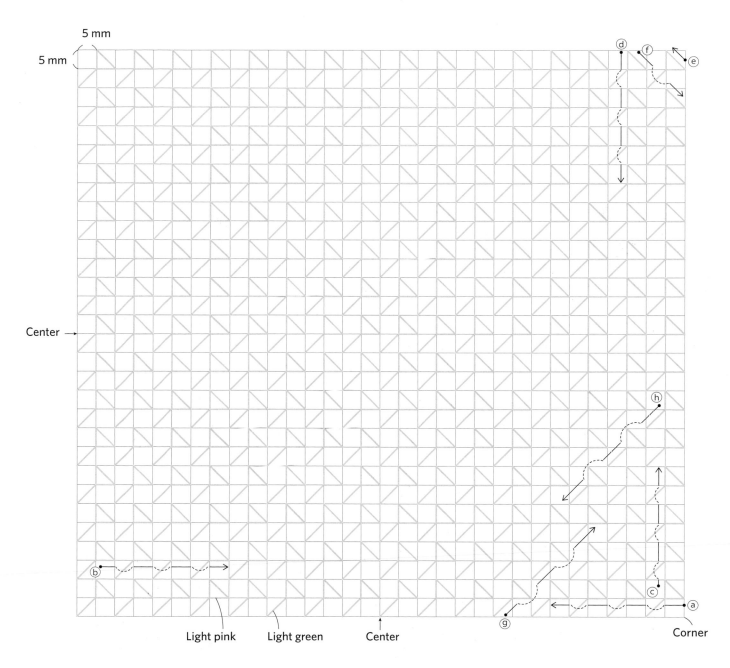

STAR LUNCH BAG

SHOWN ON PAGE 20

MATERIALS

+ OUTSIDE FABRIC: 12 × 20 in (30 × 50 cm) of light beige linen
+ LINING FABRIC: 12 × 25½ in (30 × 65 cm) of dark beige linen
+ LINEN CORD: 63 in (160 cm) of ⅜ in (8 mm) wide cord
+ Thick sashiko thread in dark pink

INSTRUCTIONS

1 Cut an 11¾ × 19 in (30 × 48 cm) rectangle of light beige linen for the bag outside. Fold in half with right sides together. On the wrong side of the fabric, mark the finishing lines ⅜ in (1 cm) from the sides. Next, mark 2½ in (6 cm) squares at the bottom corners, measuring from the finishing lines. Cut out the corners, leaving ⅜ in (1 cm) seam allowance from the marked lines. Transfer the sashiko template on page 101 onto the fabric in the area noted below.

2 Stitch the motif as noted on page 101. Make sure to stitch the motif on both the front and back.

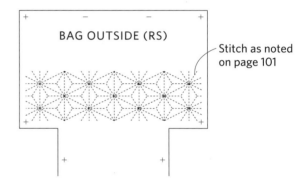

BAG OUTSIDE (RS)

Stitch as noted on page 101

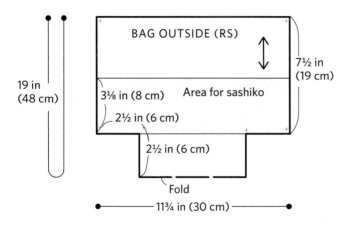

BAG OUTSIDE (RS)

7½ in (19 cm)

19 in (48 cm)

3⅛ in (8 cm)   Area for sashiko

2½ in (6 cm)

2½ in (6 cm)

Fold

11¾ in (30 cm)

3 Fold the bag outside in half with right sides together. Sew together along the sides using ⅜ in (1 cm) seam allowance. Press the side seam allowances open.

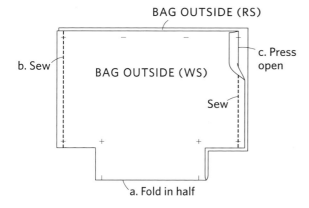

BAG OUTSIDE (RS)

BAG OUTSIDE (WS)

b. Sew

c. Press open

Sew

a. Fold in half

4 Cut an 11¾ × 25¼ in (30 × 64 cm) rectangle of dark beige linen for the lining. Fold in half with right sides together. On the wrong side of the fabric, mark the finishing lines ⅜ in (1 cm) from the sides and top. Next, mark 2½ in (6 cm) squares at the bottom corners, measuring from the finishing lines. Cut out the corners, leaving ⅜ in (1 cm) seam allowance from the marked lines. Finally, starting from the top, measure down 1⅜ in (3.5 cm) and mark a 1¼ in (3 cm) opening on each side. These will be used for inserting the drawstrings.

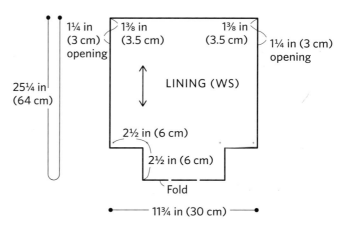

1¼ in (3 cm) opening

1⅜ in (3.5 cm)

1⅜ in (3.5 cm)

1¼ in (3 cm) opening

25¼ in (64 cm)

LINING (WS)

2½ in (6 cm)

2½ in (6 cm)

Fold

11¾ in (30 cm)

5 Fold the lining in half with right sides together. Sew together along the sides using ⅜ in (1 cm) seam allowance. Remember to leave a 1¼ in (3 cm) opening along each side as marked in step 4. Press the seam allowances open.

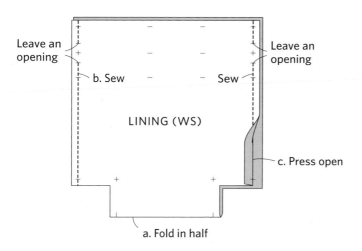

Leave an opening

b. Sew

Sew

Leave an opening

c. Press open

LINING (WS)

a. Fold in half

6 Topstitch around the drawstring openings using ⅛ in (3 mm) seam allowance.

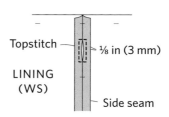

Topstitch

⅛ in (3 mm)

LINING (WS)

Side seam

7 Miter the corners on both the bag outside and lining: Align each side seam with the bottom fold of the bag to create a triangular corner. Sew across the base of each triangle with a 4¾ in (12 cm) long seam.

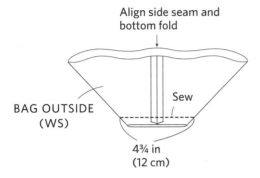

Align side seam and bottom fold

BAG OUTSIDE (WS)

Sew

4¾ in (12 cm)

8 Turn the bag outside right side out. Fold and press the top edge over ⅜ in (1 cm) to the wrong side. Fold and press the top edge of the lining over 2 in (5 cm) to the wrong side. Insert the lining into the bag outside with wrong sides together.

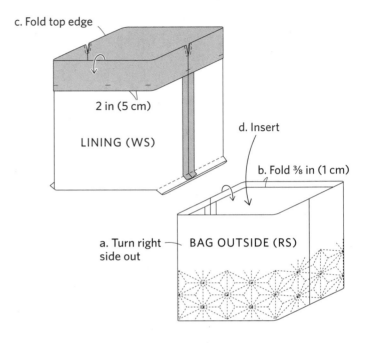

c. Fold top edge

2 in (5 cm)

LINING (WS)

d. Insert

b. Fold ⅜ in (1 cm)

a. Turn right side out

BAG OUTSIDE (RS)

9 The lining will extend 1½ in (4 cm) above the bag outside at the top. Topstitch around the bag opening, stitching ¾ in (2 cm) from the top and then ⅛ in (3 mm) below where the bag outside overlaps the lining.

a. Topstitch

LINING (RS)

¾ in (2 cm)

1½ in (4 cm)

b. Topstitch

⅛ in (3 mm)

BAG OUTSIDE (RS)

10 Cut two 31½ in (80 cm) pieces of cord. Insert each piece through the drawstring casing in opposite directions and tie the ends into a knot.

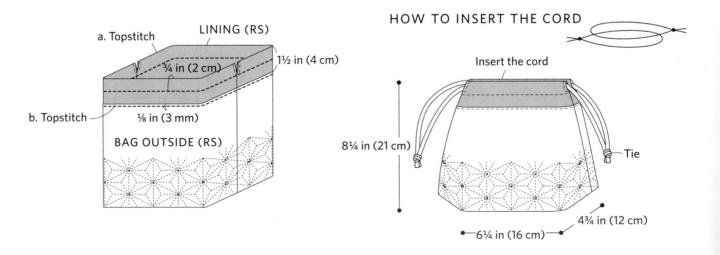

HOW TO INSERT THE CORD

Insert the cord

8¼ in (21 cm)

Tie

6¼ in (16 cm)

4¾ in (12 cm)

SASHIKO DIAGRAM

+ For best results, draw 4 x 2 cm grids. If you prefer to work in inches, draw 1½ x ¾ in grids, but please note that you may have to adjust the pattern as the resulting motif will have fewer repeats than pictured here.

+ Stitch using a single strand of sashiko thread.

+ Stitch following the alphabetical order noted in the diagram.

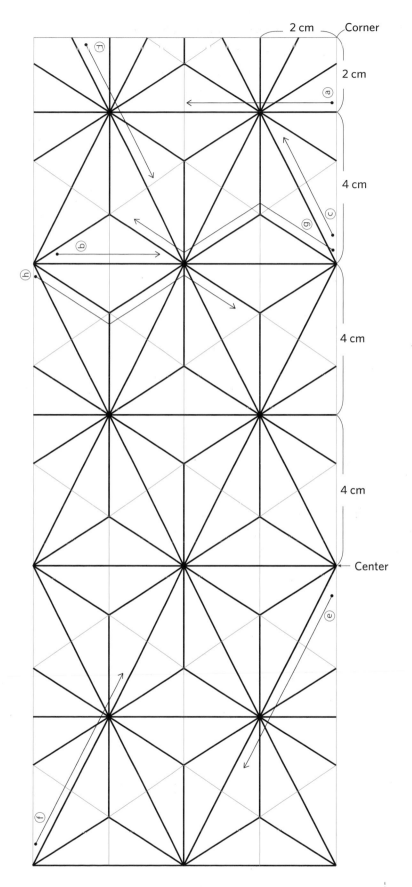

METAL CLASP COIN PURSE  SHOWN ON PAGE 21

INSTRUCTIONS

1 Use the template on page 104 to cut the purse outside out of blue linen. Mark 4 mm square grid lines on the front and stitch the motif as noted on page 104. Use the template to cut out the fusible fleece and adhere to the wrong side.

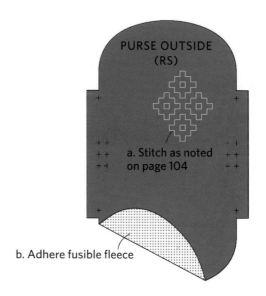

PURSE OUTSIDE
(RS)

a. Stitch as noted
on page 104

b. Adhere fusible fleece

2 Fold the purse outside in half with right sides together. Sew together along the sides using ¼ in (7 mm) seam allowance. Make clips into the seam allowance just above the ends of the seams.

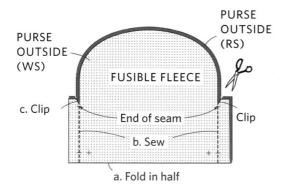

PURSE
OUTSIDE
(WS)

PURSE
OUTSIDE
(RS)

FUSIBLE FLEECE

c. Clip

End of seam

Clip

b. Sew

a. Fold in half

3 Press the seam allowances open. Fold and press the seam allowance to the wrong side at the clipped areas. Use the template to cut a lining out of striped cotton. Repeat steps 2 and 3 to sew the lining.

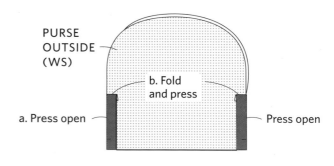

PURSE
OUTSIDE
(WS)

b. Fold
and press

a. Press open

Press open

4 Sew the mitered corners on both the purse and lining: Align each side seam with the bottom fold of the purse to create a triangular corner. Sew across the base of each triangle with a ⅝ in (1.4 cm) long seam.

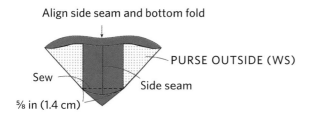

Align side seam and bottom fold

PURSE OUTSIDE (WS)

Sew

Side seam

⅝ in (1.4 cm)

5 Turn the purse right side out. Insert the lining into the purse with wrong sides together. Sew together around the purse opening, stitching ¹⁄₁₆ in (2 mm) from the edge.

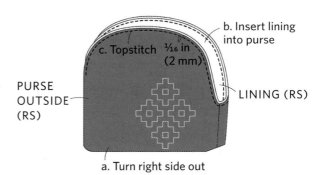

b. Insert lining into purse

c. Topstitch ¹⁄₁₆ in (2 mm)

PURSE OUTSIDE (RS)

LINING (RS)

a. Turn right side out

6 Use a toothpick to apply glue to the channel on one half of the clasp. Use a screwdriver or stiletto to insert one half of the purse into the clasp. Next, cut the paper string in half to match the length of each side of the clasp. Insert a piece of paper string into the channel to help hold the fabric in place. Finally, use pliers and a scrap of batting to squeeze the clasp just above each hinge. Repeat process to install the other half of the clasp.

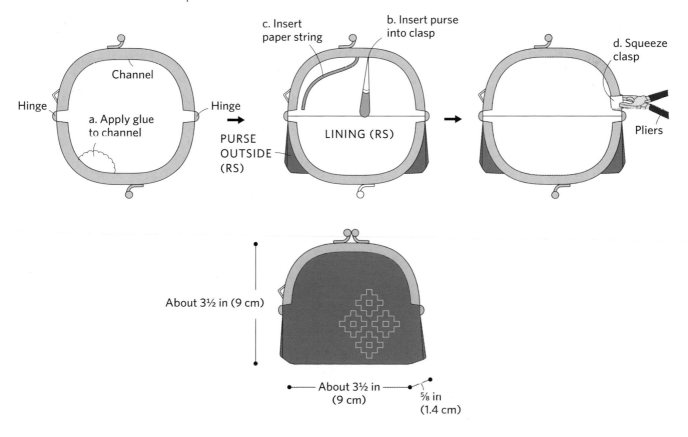

Channel

Hinge

Hinge

a. Apply glue to channel

PURSE OUTSIDE (RS)

c. Insert paper string

b. Insert purse into clasp

LINING (RS)

d. Squeeze clasp

Pliers

About 3½ in (9 cm)

About 3½ in (9 cm)

⅝ in (1.4 cm)

SASHIKO DIAGRAM
& FULL SIZE TEMPLATE

+ For best results, draw 4 mm grids. If you prefer to work in inches, draw ⅛ in grids, but please note that you may have to adjust the pattern as the resulting motif will have fewer repeats than pictured here.

+ Stitch using a single strand of sashiko thread.

+ Stitch following the alphabetical order noted in the diagram.

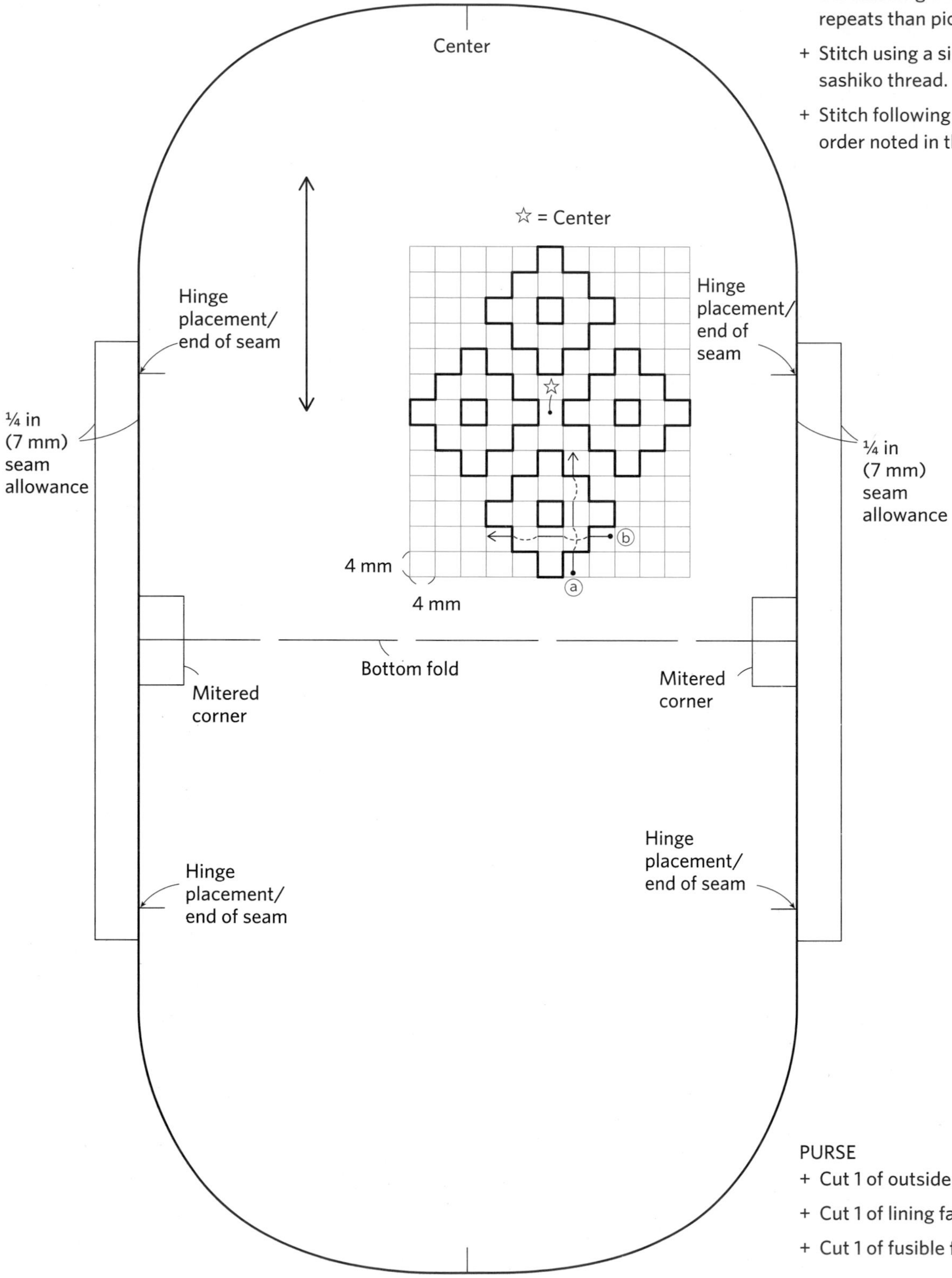

Center

☆ = Center

Hinge placement/ end of seam

Hinge placement/ end of seam

¼ in (7 mm) seam allowance

¼ in (7 mm) seam allowance

4 mm

4 mm

ⓐ

ⓑ

Bottom fold

Mitered corner

Mitered corner

Hinge placement/ end of seam

Hinge placement/ end of seam

PURSE
+ Cut 1 of outside fabric
+ Cut 1 of lining fabric
+ Cut 1 of fusible fleece

RUNNING STITCH HAND TOWEL

SHOWN ON PAGE 22

MATERIALS

+ FABRIC: 13½ × 27½ in (34 × 70 cm) of unbleached cotton muslin
+ Sashiko thread in turquoise and yellow

INSTRUCTIONS

1 Fold the fabric in half lengthwise with right sides together. Sew together along the top using ⅜ in (1 cm) seam allowance. Trim the seam allowance to ¼ in (7 mm).

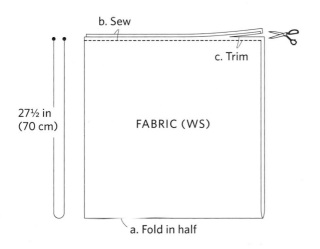

b. Sew

c. Trim

27½ in (70 cm)

FABRIC (WS)

a. Fold in half

2 Turn right side out. Starting at the corner, work running stitch around the perimeter using turquoise thread, stitching ¼ in (5 mm) from the edge. Next, work another round of running stitch using yellow thread, stitching ¼ in (5 mm) from the turquoise round. Stitch through both layers of fabric on both rounds.

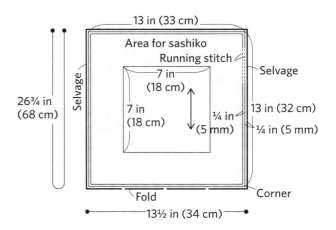

13 in (33 cm)

Area for sashiko

Running stitch

Selvage

7 in (18 cm)

7 in (18 cm)

¼ in (5 mm)

26¾ in (68 cm)

Selvage

13 in (32 cm)

¼ in (5 mm)

Fold

Corner

13½ in (34 cm)

3 Mark 5 mm square grid lines on the fabric and stitch the motif as noted on page 106.

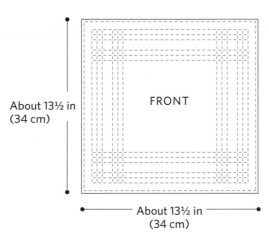

About 13½ in (34 cm)

FRONT

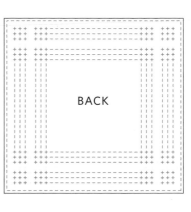

BACK

About 13½ in (34 cm)

SASHIKO DIAGRAM

+ For best results, draw 5 mm grids. If you prefer to work in inches, draw ¼ in grids, but please note that you may have to adjust the pattern as the resulting motif will have fewer repeats than pictured here.

+ Stitch using a single strand of sashiko thread.

+ Stitch following the alphabetical order noted in the diagram. Pass the thread between the two layers of fabric when moving from row ⓒ to ⓓ and from row ⓔ to ⓕ.

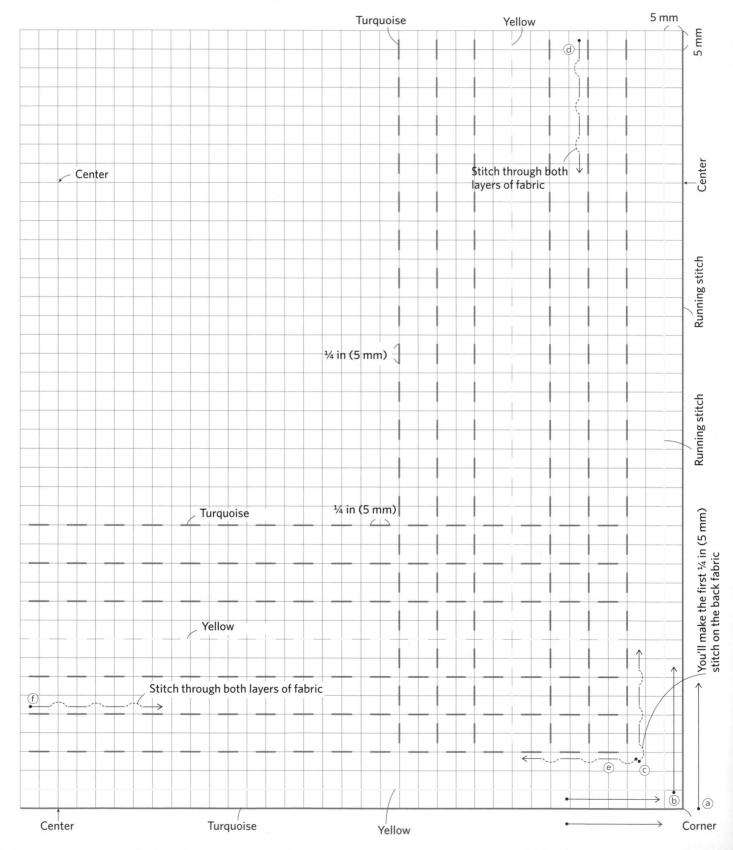

LEAF HAND TOWEL

SHOWN ON PAGE 25

MATERIALS

+ FABRIC: 14¼ in (36 cm) square of light blue textured linen

+ Thick sashiko thread in yellow and teal

INSTRUCTIONS

1 Mark 4.1 cm square grid lines on the fabric and stitch the motif as noted on page 108. Once the stitching is complete, hem the towel by folding the raw edges over ¼ in (7 mm) and then ⅜ in (8 mm), mitering the corners as shown.

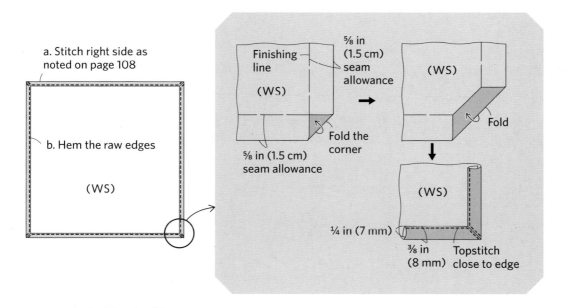

a. Stitch right side as noted on page 108

b. Hem the raw edges

(WS)

Finishing line

(WS)

⅝ in (1.5 cm) seam allowance

⅝ in (1.5 cm) seam allowance

Fold the corner

(WS)

Fold

(WS)

¼ in (7 mm)

⅜ in (8 mm)

Topstitch close to edge

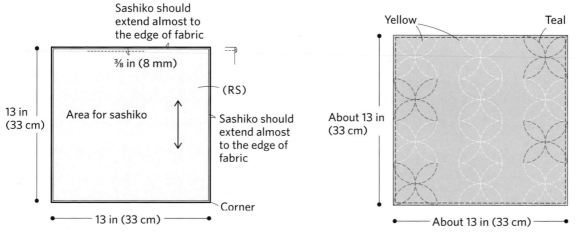

Sashiko should extend almost to the edge of fabric

⅜ in (8 mm)

(RS)

Area for sashiko

13 in (33 cm)

Sashiko should extend almost to the edge of fabric

13 in (33 cm)

Corner

Yellow

Teal

About 13 in (33 cm)

About 13 in (33 cm)

SASHIKO DIAGRAM

+ For best results, draw 4.1 cm grids. If you prefer to work in inches, draw 1½ in grids, but please note that you may have to adjust the pattern as the resulting motif will have fewer repeats than pictured here.

+ Stitch using a single strand of sashiko thread.

+ Stitch following the alphabetical order noted in the diagram.

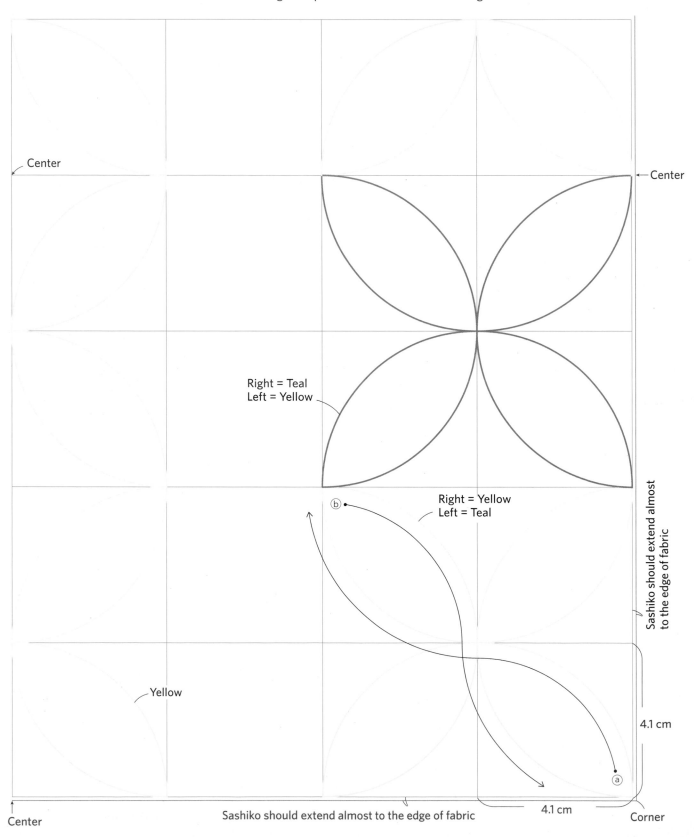

Center

Center

Right = Teal
Left = Yellow

Right = Yellow
Left = Teal

ⓑ

Yellow

Sashiko should extend almost to the edge of fabric

4.1 cm

ⓐ

Center

Sashiko should extend almost to the edge of fabric

4.1 cm

Corner

PICNIC BASKET CLOTH

SHOWN ON PAGE 24

MATERIALS

+ FRONT FABRIC: 20 in (50 cm) square of checkered linen (look for a checkered fabric with ⅜ in [8 mm] squares)
+ BACK FABRIC: 20 in (50 cm) square of mustard linen
+ Thick sashiko thread in tan

INSTRUCTIONS

1 Cut one 19 in (48.4 cm) square out of the checkered linen for the front and one out of the mustard linen for the back. Align the front and back with right sides together. Sew together around all four sides using ⅜ in (1 cm) seam allowance, but leave two 5 in (13 cm) openings along the bottom as shown. Trim the corner seam allowances at an angle.

FRONT (RS)

⅜ in (1 cm)

b. Trim the corners

a. Sew

BACK (WS)

Leave an opening   Leave an opening

2 in (5 cm)   4 in (10 cm)   2 in (5 cm)

2 Turn right side out. Thread the needle with sashiko thread and make a knot at the end. Use the right opening to insert the needle between the two layers of fabric. Bring the needle up to the top right corner and draw the needle out on the back. Make the first ¼ in (5 mm) horizontal stitch. This will be the horizontal part of the first cross. Draw the needle out on the front.

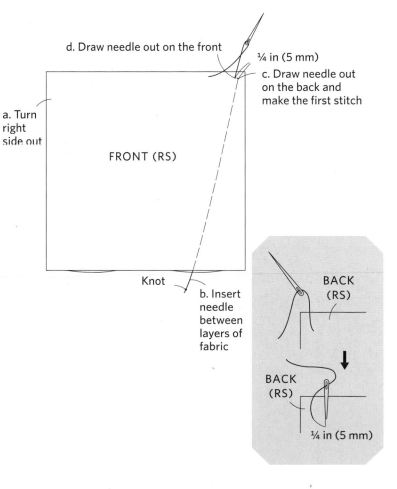

d. Draw needle out on the front

¼ in (5 mm)

c. Draw needle out on the back and make the first stitch

a. Turn right side out

FRONT (RS)

Knot

b. Insert needle between layers of fabric

BACK (RS)

BACK (RS)

¼ in (5 mm)

3 Mark 8 mm grid lines on the fabric in the area noted below or use the checkered pattern of the fabric as a guide. Stitch the front motif as noted on page 111. Note: This motif was designed for checkered fabric with ⅜ in (8 mm) squares. Adjust the motif as necessary if using checkered fabric with different sized squares. The cross pattern will form on the back as you stitch the front. When the stitching is complete, draw the needle out through the left opening.

1 square of the checkered
pattern = ⅜ in (8 mm)

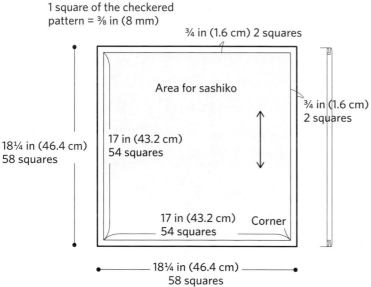

¾ in (1.6 cm) 2 squares

Area for sashiko

¾ in (1.6 cm)
2 squares

17 in (43.2 cm)
54 squares

18¼ in (46.4 cm)
58 squares

17 in (43.2 cm)
54 squares

Corner

18¼ in (46.4 cm)
58 squares

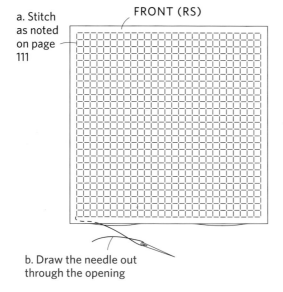

FRONT (RS)

a. Stitch as noted on page 111

b. Draw the needle out through the opening

4 Hand stitch the openings closed.

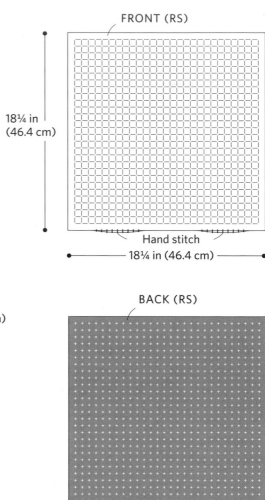

FRONT (RS)

18¼ in
(46.4 cm)

Hand stitch

18¼ in (46.4 cm)

BACK (RS)

SASHIKO DIAGRAM

+ For best results, draw 8 mm grids. If you prefer to work in inches, draw ⅜ in grids, but please note that you may have to adjust the pattern as the resulting motif will have fewer repeats than pictured here.

+ Stitch using a single strand of sashiko thread.

+ Stitch following the alphabetical order noted in the diagram. Pass the thread between the two layers of fabric when moving from row ⓐ to ⓑ and from row ⓒ to ⓓ.

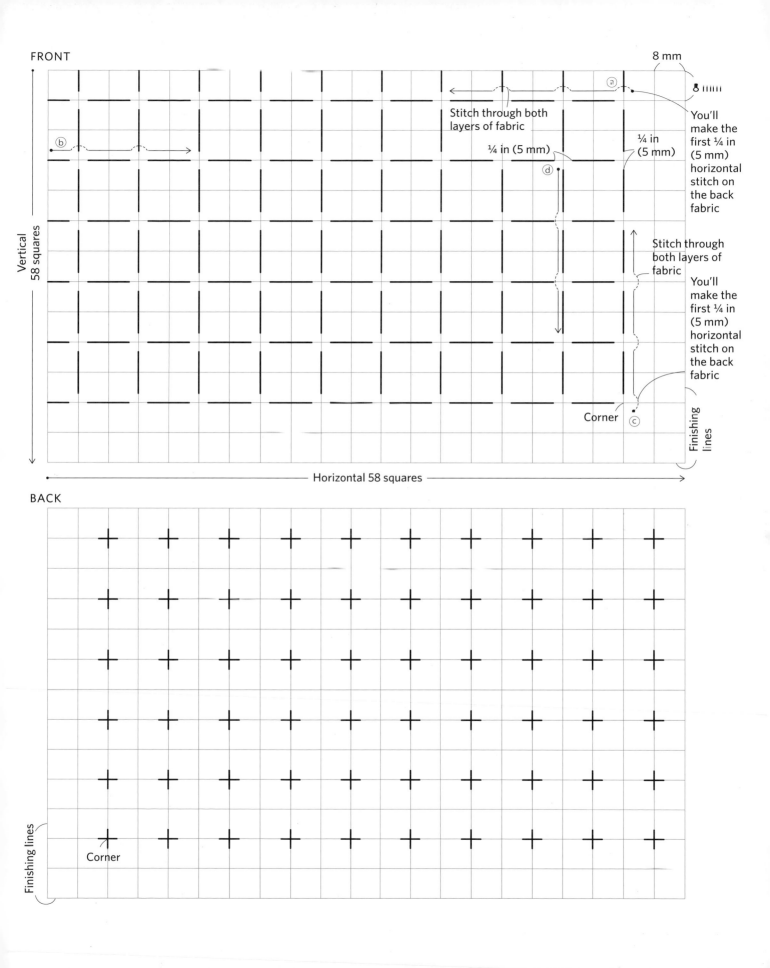

FRONT

Vertical 58 squares

Horizontal 58 squares

8 mm

Stitch through both layers of fabric

You'll make the first ¼ in (5 mm) horizontal stitch on the back fabric

¼ in (5 mm)

¼ in (5 mm)

Stitch through both layers of fabric

You'll make the first ¼ in (5 mm) horizontal stitch on the back fabric

Corner

Finishing lines

ⓐ ⓑ ⓒ ⓓ

BACK

Finishing lines

Corner

RESOURCES

A THREADED NEEDLE

WWW.ATHREADEDNEEDLE.COM

Canadian site that carries a wide assortment of sashiko threads in different weights and colors, as well as fabric, needles, and notions.

BEBE BOLD

WWW.BEBEBOLD.COM

Australian site with an extensive selection of sashiko tools and materials.

PURL SOHO

WWW.PURLSOHO.COM

Sells a variety of colorful sashiko threads, as well as needles and thimbles. Shop online or visit their NYC location.

SHIBORI DRAGON

WWW.SHIBORIDRAGON.COM

Online source for sashiko thread, fabric, and notions.

STITCHED MODERN

WWW.STITCHEDMODERN.COM

Online site with lots of different colors of sashiko threads plus notions.